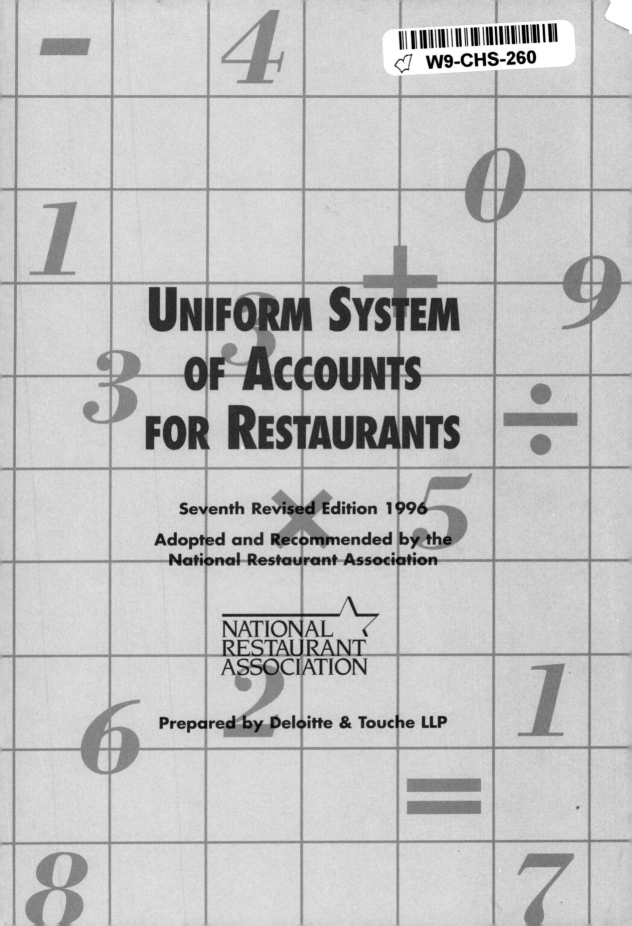

# UNIFORM SYSTEM OF ACCOUNTS FOR RESTAURANTS

Seventh Revised Edition 1996

Adopted and Recommended by the
National Restaurant Association

NATIONAL
RESTAURANT
ASSOCIATION

Prepared by Deloitte & Touche LLP

# Table of Contents

# Preface

The board of directors of the National Restaurant Association is gratified that the book Uniform System of Accounts for Restaurants has proven over the years to be the association's "best seller." More important, this continuing demand has been evidence that its membership appreciates the assistance this publication has given to restaurant operators in creating a common language for the industry, based on an intelligent means of analyzing their results. It also has given restaurant owners and operators wider opportunity to compare their figures with those of others in the business and with the published results of restaurant studies conducted by the association , such as its annual Restaurant Industry Operations Survey.

In response to restaurant operators' demand for authentic data on operating results and guidance on their financial problems, this edition has followed the pattern used in previous editions and again contains detailed explanations of the suggested classification of accounts and samples of balance sheets and income statements, illustrating their practicality and use. For the first time, a comprehensive expense dictionary is also included to assist restaurant operators in classifying the many expenses associated with their operations.

Although this is a veritable textbook for the restaurant operator on the subject of restaurant accounting,  its primary objective is to help operators of smaller restaurants interpret their results and financial positions. At the same time, it gives consideration to how the Uniform System can be used to advantage by operators of the large restaurants.

It is the hope of the board of directors that the members of the National Restaurant Association will continue to benefit in their own operations from the general adoption of the Uniform System of Accounts for Restaurants and, as a corollary, from the wealth of reliable data from future studies and published figures based on its use that will be available for comparison with their operations.

## For further information

The National Restaurant Association's Research and Information Services Department offers a broad array of additional publications and services that may assist you and your business, such as:

**Research Studies**—unique surveys and analyses of topics relating to restaurants, ranging from operational results and wages and benefits to consumer demand and trends.

**Foodservice Trends**—analysis and interpretation of industry research appearing monthly in Restaurants USA.

**How-To Manuals**—a series of publications on critical aspects of running a restaurant, including accounting, hiring, marketing, preparing a business plan and other topics.

**Consultant and Software Databases**—computerized listings of consultants and software vendors that serve the restaurant industry.

For further information, call the Association's Research and Information Services Department at (800) 424-5156 or (202) 331-5960.

# Foreword

To:        Membership of the National Restaurant Association

From:    Deloitte & Touche LLP

Ladies and Gentlemen:

The purpose of this text is to introduce the reader to a standard accounting classification system usable by most restaurant operators. This is not an accounting text or operations manual, nor a guide for compliance with the requirements of the Securities and Exchange Commission, but an introduction to a standardized accounting system, restaurant controls and record keeping, and relevant income tax matters. We believe this text is most helpful to sole proprietors and partnerships owning a limited number of restaurants.

The organization of the system and the classification of accounts have changed little since this manual was last published. However, updated terminology has been included, as well as current accounting treatment of various transactions and some modifications in the presentation of accounts within the statement of income. We have also introduced comments on budgeting and budgetary control, ratio analysis and tax considerations to provide the reader with additional tools to manage his or her restaurant business. Appendix B contains an Expense Dictionary designed to assist in the classification of expenses in accordance with the *Uniform System of Accounts for Restaurants*.

We hope this text is useful to you and that it contributes to the success of your restaurant business. We extend our thanks to the National Restaurant Association for the opportunity to be involved in this project, as well as for their cooperation and advice in preparing this edition of the *Uniform System of Accounts for Restaurants*.

Very truly yours,
Deloitte & Touche LLP

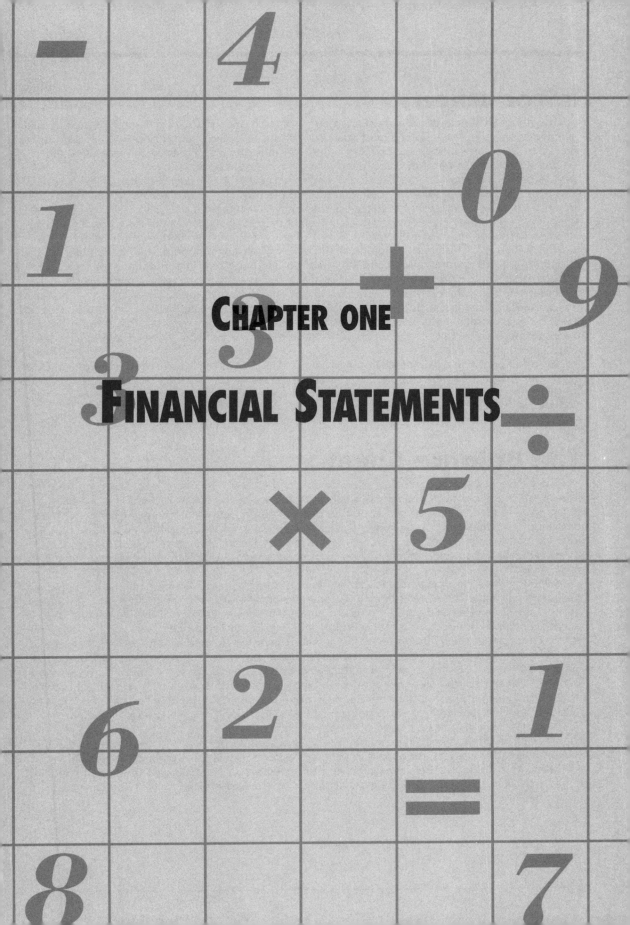

# CHAPTER ONE

# FINANCIAL STATEMENTS

# Introduction

The financial statements of a business consist of a balance sheet, a statement of income and retained earnings, and a statement of cash flows that shows the sources and uses of cash. In the interest of consistency, each is discussed in this text in sequence; however, the statement of income will probably be of the most interest to the restaurant operator.

The primary purpose of the *Uniform System of Accounts for Restaurants* (the Uniform System) is to give restaurant operators a common language to use in their accounting statements, so when they discuss their businesses with other operators, they will know that each is talking about the same thing when they mention food costs or direct operating expenses. At the same time, this common language must take the form that will give the majority of restaurant operators a clear picture of the major elements of their business, showing how each major item contributes to it. By its use, restaurant operators will have the benefit of the analytical interpretation and experience of accountants in the presentation of their own figures. They will also get an extra dividend because they can compare their operations intelligently with the statements of others in the restaurant business and with the published figures made available to them through their trade associations, trade periodicals and special studies covering the restaurant field. As the Uniform System becomes more universally adopted, operators can make comparisons without having to make adjustments.

An additional benefit of the Uniform System is that it gives third-party users of financial statements (such as lenders) the opportunity to compare a restaurant operator's statements with industry averages. Such comparisons are greatly facilitated when industry averages and the operator's statements share a common format.

# The Balance Sheet

The balance sheet presents the historical cost of the assets, liabilities and debts, and owner's investment of the business; it presents a summary picture of the business' financial condition at a given point in time. The financial condition of a restaurant depends on many factors, such as the amount of investment of the owners, the ability to obtain borrowed capital, the attitude of creditors, the ability of the operator to penetrate the market, the location and local economic conditions. Implementation and maintenance of proper records are essential to preparation of a balance sheet.

Although the form of the balance sheet of a restaurant is made up in much the same manner as that of any other business, it highlights some major differences. For example, a restaurant ordinarily does not extend wide credit to its customers and thus does not have large sums tied up in accounts receivable nor does it require a large investment in inventories. Instead, the usual restaurant balance sheet shows that most of the money is invested in fixed assets, such as land, buildings, furniture, equipment, leasehold and leasehold improvements. The working capital requirement is also smaller than that of a manufacturing business because, for the most part, restaurant sales are either immediately realized in cash or are charged to credit cards and quickly converted to cash. Since the restaurant operator may obtain credit in the payment of bills, it is possible to make payment on some of the expenses for last month with the cash taken in today.

Exhibit A demonstrates the form of a balance sheet, including accounts common to restaurants. Each of the balance sheet elements will be explained briefly. Not all of these accounts will be necessary in every restaurant, and some restaurants will have other accounts which are not listed. This balance sheet reflects the recommendations of the American Institute of Certified Public Accounts with respect to the classification of current assets and current liabilities as of December 31, 1994.

Exhibit A

# Balance Sheet
# Name of Restaurant Company as of (Insert Date)

| **Current Assets** | **Assets** | |
|---|---|---|
| Cash on Hand | $ 15,000 | |
| Cash in Banks | 710,000 | $ 725,000 |
| | | |
| Accounts Receivable: | | |
| Trade | 17,000 | |
| Employees | 9,000 | |
| Other | 2,000 | |
| Total Receivables | 28,000 | |
| Deduct Allowance for Doubtful Accounts | (1,000) | 27,000 |
| | | |
| Inventories: | | |
| Food | 375,000 | |
| Beverages | 55,000 | |
| Gift and Sundry Shop | 8,000 | |
| Supplies | 2,000 | 440,000 |
| Prepaid Expenses | | 250,000 |
| **Total Current Assets** | | **1,442,000** |
| | | |
| Due from officers, stockholders, partners and employees | | 5,000 |
| Due from affiliated or associated companies | | 1,000 |
| Cash held by trustee—restricted | | 4,000 |
| | | |
| FIXED ASSETS: | | |
| Land | 50,000 | |
| Buildings | 250,000 | |
| Cost of Improvements in Progress | 15,000 | |
| Leasehold and Leasehold Improvements | 40,000 | |
| Furniture, Fixtures and Equipment | 12,000 | |
| Uniforms, Linens, China, Glass, Silver, Utensils | 9,000 | |
| Deduct Accumulated Depreciation and Amortization | (125,000) | |
| Net Book Value of Fixed Assets | | 251,000 |
| | | |
| DEFERRED EXPENSES: | | |
| Organization and Pre-opening Expenses | 4,000 | |
| Bond Discount and Loan Initiation Fees | 6,000 | 10,000 |
| | | |
| OTHER ASSETS: | | |
| Amount Paid for Goodwill | 10,000 | |
| Cost of Bar License | 20,000 | |
| Rental Deposits | 8,000 | |
| Cash Surrender Value of Life Insurance | 5,000 | |
| Deposit on Franchise or Royalty Contract | 25,000 | 68,000 |
| | | |
| **TOTAL ASSETS** | | **$1,781,000** |

# Liabilities and Shareholders' Equity

## Current Liabilities

| | | |
|---|---:|---:|
| Accounts Payable: | | |
| Trade | $1,379,000 | |
| Others | 4,000 | $1,383,000 |
| | | |
| Notes Payable—Banks | | 15,000 |
| Taxes Collected | | 4,000 |
| Accrued Expenses: | | |
| Salaries and Wages | 9,000 | |
| Payroll Taxes | 2,000 | |
| Real Estate and Personal Property Taxes | 6,000 | |
| Rent | 8,000 | |
| Interest | 3,000 | |
| Utilities | 1,000 | |
| Other | 1,000 | 30,000 |
| | | |
| Employees' Deposits | | 1,000 |
| Deposits on Banquets | | 1,000 |
| Income Taxes—State and Federal | | 7,000 |
| Current Portion of Long-Term Debt | | 15,000 |
| Dividends Declared and Payable | | 10,000 |
| **Total Current Liabilities** | | **1,466,000** |
| | | |
| Due to officers, stockholders, partners | | 1,000 |
| Due to affliliated or associated companies | | 2,000 |
| Long-term debt, net of current portion | | 30,000 |
| Deferred income taxes | | 9,000 |
| Other noncurrent liabilities | | 7,000 |
| **TOTAL LIABILITIES** | | **1,515,000** |
| | | |
| SHAREHOLDERS' EQUITY (if a Corporation): | | |
| Capital Stock | 5,000 | |
| Description of Each Type of Stock, | | |
| Shares Authorized and Issued, | | |
| Stated Value per Share | | |
| Paid-in Capital | 120,000 | |
| Retained Earnings | 141,000 | |
| Total Shareholders' Equity | 266,000 | |
| | | |
| NET WORTH (if an Individual Proprietor or Partnership): | | |
| Proprietor's Account | 266,000 | |
| Partner A | 133,000 | |
| Partner B | 133,000 | |
| Total Net Worth | 266,000 | |
| | | |
| **TOTAL LIABILITIES AND CAPITAL** | | **$1,781,000** |

Note:  Numbers used are for illustrative purposes only.

# Current Assets

The current assets accounts include cash, receivables, inventories of saleable food, merchandise and supplies, marketable securities and prepaid expenses.

## Cash on Hand

This account reflects the house funds, house banks or change funds in the custody of cashiers or other employees of the restaurant.

If all cash receipts are deposited daily, as advocated later in this book, the undeposited receipts, which may temporarily be on hand at the end of the month, will be included in cash in banks as deposits in transit in the month-end bank reconciliation.

## Cash in Banks

Cash in banks reflects the total of the book balances of all bank accounts, including cash which is immediately available from the deposit or electronic transfer of credit card receipts. If more than one bank account is maintained, each bank account will, of course, require a separate account in the accounting records of the restaurant.

If cash is deposited in a special account to be used for a specific purpose and not in the ordinary course of business and thus is not available for the liquidation of current liabilities, the account should be shown under a separate heading in the non-current assets. Such restricted cash might be deposited to a sinking fund required under a mortgage or put in escrow to fund the purchase of assets or liquidation of liabilities.

## Receivables

This account should be charged with all amounts due from customers on open account and amounts due from credit card companies. An operator may wish to separate the amounts due to extension of credit to regular customers from those which arise from the policy of accepting credit cards. Employees' and officers' current balances due, rentals or commissions from concessionaires, and accounts rising from temporary loans to employees come under this category. Amounts due from officers, employees and other related parties should be shown separately or disclosed in the footnotes.

In the event the restaurant should have a current obligation due to it which is covered by a note, it should be listed in a separate note receivable account, and the amount of the note should be shown as a separate item with the receivables.

Notes and accounts due from stockholders, officers, employees and affiliated or associated enterprises which are not due within one year from the date of the balance sheet should not be included under this caption but should be shown separately on the balance sheet below the total of current assets.

The detail of accounts and notes receivables, showing the names of the debtors, the age of the accounts and the individual amounts due, may be shown in a supporting schedule to the balance sheet. The extent of this detail will depend on the individual requirements of the person for whom the statements are prepared.

## Allowance for Doubtful Accounts

An allowance for probable losses in the collection of existing receivables should be provided, and this account should be credited with an amount sufficient to cover accounts that are considered doubtful. If this is done monthly, the charge to expense which is to be credited to this account is usually based on past experience, and the amount is adjusted to the actual collectibility of the accounts at the end of the year.

When this method is used, any uncollectible accounts should be charged to the allowance account when they are written off. Allowances are adjusted by the bookkeeper monthly through journal entries.

## Inventories

A separate account should be kept for each type of inventory. The food inventory will include the cost of provisions that are on hand in the storeroom, refrigerators, pantries, kitchens and in storage warehouses. The beverage inventory will include stock at the bars or in the storeroom, wine cellar and warehouses. There should be other inventory accounts for the gift and sundry shop, other merchandise intended for sale and supplies used in the business, such as cleaning supplies and mechanical supplies.

Because of the rapid turnover of these items, it is usual to value the inventories of a restaurant at the latest cost of each item, unless material discrepancies would result.

Linens, china, glass, silver, utensils and uniforms are classified as fixed assets under the Uniform System. For that reason, any amounts shown in the inventory accounts that are kept on these items are not included here with the current assets but are shown in the later section of the balance sheet devoted to fixed assets.

## Prepaid Expenses

A separate account should be kept for each prepaid expense item. Generally, all prepaid items should be listed on the face of the balance sheet as a single line item. They may be shown in more detail in a supporting schedule. This group of assets includes such items as unexpired insurance premiums, prepaid interest, rent, taxes and licenses.

## Total Current Assets

The balance sheet should show a total of current assets. The operator will then know the liquid or current position of the company in determining its working capital and current ratio (discussed later in this chapter), which are important factors in indicating the ability to meet current bills.

## Due from Officers, Stockholders, Partners and Employees

Receivables due from officers, stockholders, partners and employees, including loans or notes and accrued interest thereon that are not collectible within one year of the date of the balance sheet, should be shown as separate items below the total of current assets on the balance sheet. Repayment terms, interest rates, collateral and other pertinent information should be disclosed in the footnotes.

## Due from Affiliated or Associated Companies

The same treatment should be given to amounts due from affiliated or associated companies as is suggested for amounts due from officers, stockholders, partners and employees.

## Cash Held by Trustee—Restricted

Cash deposited with a trustee or placed in escrow, which is thus restricted in nature and not available for the payment of liabilities incurred in the ordinary daily course of business, should be shown separately on the balance sheet below the total of current assets. If, however, such cash is deposited with trustees for the payment of current obligations which are shown in the current liability section of the balance sheet, they may be shown as current assets. Such items may be current interest and principal payments on a loan or real estate taxes.

## Fixed Assets

This class of assets, which is to be shown as a separate group on the balance sheet below the total of current assets, includes items used in the business, such as land, buildings, furniture, fixtures and equipment, automobiles and trucks, and unamortized value of leaseholds and leasehold improvements and purchased computer hardware and software. There should be a separate account for each type of fixed asset.

The basis of value, which is generally historical cost, should be shown on the face of the balance sheet. Buildings, furniture, fixtures and equipment, and automobiles and trucks are subject to evaluation based on their age and the estimate of the extent of their useful life that has expired. This is done by creating an accumulated depreciation account for each type. Generally, the accumulated depreciation accounts for each asset are combined on the balance sheet. In case of a leasehold or leasehold improvement, the value decreases as the lease expires. This decrease in value is also reflected in an accumulated amortization account which is deducted from the respective asset to reflect the extent to which its value has been charged to operations. This accumulated amortization account is also combined with accumulated depreciation when presented on the face of the balance sheet. Thus, the amount of these asset accounts minus the amount of their accumulated depreciation or amortization leaves the net asset value remaining to be charged to future operations in the ordinary course of business.

These accumulated depreciation and amortization accounts are merely a means of spreading the cost of the asset over the term of its useful life, and they are not an attempt to establish the true or saleable value of the asset at any given time. Thus, these accounts reflect what is known as a book value, which is not to be confused with market or net realizable value.

The accounts representing asset values of linen, china, glass, silver, utensils and uniforms are also to be included under fixed assets. These items may or may not be accounted for by periodical inventories. The procedures for charging these items to expense accounts are outlined in the section of this book describing the statement of income. The original investment is often included in the total of the furniture and fixtures account, and any replacements are charged to operating expenses as they are purchased. Generally, a reserve is created and offset against the original cost to reflect the average state of deterioration or use of the overall inventory of these items.

The cost of construction of improvements in progress should be included as a component of fixed assets. Once these improvements have been completed, they should be transferred to the buildings or leasehold improvements account, as appropriate. At this time, depreciation or amortization of these improvements should begin.

## Deferred Expenses

Deferred expenses are to be shown on the balance sheet following the total of fixed assets. These costs include expenditures made which have no recoverable value and which are being systematically charged to expense over the estimated period benefited or costs which will subsequently be charged to a fixed-asset account. They include items such as organization and preopening expenses, bond discount and loan expenses.

In the case of a corporation, certain expenditures are required to organize the business and establish the corporation. Examples of organization costs are legal services, filing fees and stock issuance record costs. These organization costs can either be recorded as general and administrative costs when incurred or can be capitalized under other assets and amortized over a period of time, generally five years. An accumulated amortization account may be established to record the amortization, but it is usually not shown separately on the balance sheet.

Costs that are incurred prior to the opening of a restaurant, such as training of employees, can also be immediately recorded as an expense as if the restaurant were operating, or they can be recorded as an other asset and amortized over a twelve-month period. It is preferable accounting treatment to expense these costs immediately, however.

## Other Assets

Other assets include items that cannot readily be included under any other grouping in the balance sheet. They are usually shown as the last item on the asset side of this statement, and their nature should be clearly shown on the face of the balance sheet. They include items such as goodwill, bar and liquor licenses (in many states where licenses are restricted in number, it is often necessary to purchase an existing license), a deposit on utility services (such as water, gas and electricity) and the deposit on a franchise or royalty contract.

Other assets will include any deposits of cash or marketable investments required as security for building rent due and the proper performance of other stated terms. If this deposit should draw interest payable to the operator, the amount of this accrued interest receivable may be shown as a current asset.

In cases where insurance is carried on the lives of officers, partners or key employees and the company is the beneficiary under the policy, the cash surrender value as shown by the policy should be accrued as an asset with a corresponding reduction in the life insurance expense.

## Current Liabilities

The current liability section of the balance sheet includes items that become due in less than one year, such as bank overdrafts, short-term loans from banks and other loans covered by notes, open accounts payable to trade creditors and others, and taxes collected from customers and employees payable to federal or local government agencies. It also includes deposits collected to apply on future sales commitments, accrued expenses and the portion of long-term liabilities that is due within one year of the balance sheet date.

## Accounts Payable—Trade Creditors

Trade creditors are those from whom the restaurant receives goods or services in the ordinary course of business. The total of the unpaid invoices due to these creditors for all goods or services received prior to the balance sheet date is included in this caption.

## Accounts Payable—Others

Accounts due to concessionaires representing collections from customers or extraordinarily large open accounts, such as might result from purchases of equipment, will generally be shown separately on the balance sheet.

## Notes Payable

This account should include short-term notes due to banks. If there are additional short-term notes on loans from others, they should be described and shown separately. The payment terms, interest rates, collateral, restrictions and other pertinent terms should be disclosed in the footnotes.

## Taxes Collected

All taxes collected from customers and employees and payable to federal or local governmental agencies should be shown under this heading. These items include the following:

### Collected from Customers
Sales Tax—Excise tax on gift shop items

### Collected from Employees
Federal Insurance Contributions Act Tax
Federal Income Tax Withheld
State and Local Unemployment or Income Tax (where collected)

In some instances the restaurant also collects union dues and similar items payable to other than governmental agencies. The liabilities for these items are usually included in this group.

## Accrued Expenses

In many instances, expenses are incurred for a period of operation and are not payable until after the balance sheet date. Therefore, the amount of these expenses which applies to the period up to the balance sheet date is an actual current liability and should be recorded, not only to show the true picture of financial condition but also to charge each operating period with its proper proportion of these costs of doing business. These are called accrued expenses and they include:

Salaries and Wages
Earned Vacation Time and Sick Leave
Payroll Taxes
Federal Insurance Contributions Act Tax
Federal Unemployment

State Unemployment
Rent
Franchise Fee
Interest (preferably showing amount on each type of loan or note separately)
Energy and Utilities:
   Electricity
   Gas
   Water
   Telephone

Any other situation in which an expense has been incurred for goods or services received prior to the balance sheet date but an invoice has not been received should be included.

All of these accounts should be shown in one group in the current liability section and may be listed in detail in a supporting schedule.

Smaller restaurants sometimes believe that it is not practical to go to the trouble of making these entries on the theory that the amounts involved are comparatively small and their omission will not seriously distort the figures on the statement of income. However, a consistent effort to record these items will produce more accurate and useful financial information.

Many restaurants sell gift certificates which may be redeemed for food or beverages at a future date. When a gift certificate is purchased, an accrued expense account entitled gift certificates sold should be credited with the amount of the certificate sold. When the gift certificate is presented for redemption, the gift certificates sold account is relieved and the food sales account is credited with the amount of the check. It is advisable to keep an accurate log of the gift certificates available for sale and those sold but not yet redeemed and to keep the unsold certificates in a secure place.

## Employees' Deposits

Some restaurants control uniforms, badges and other similar articles put into the custody of employees by obtaining a deposit for them, to be returned when the article is returned. These deposits should also appear as a current liability on the balance sheet.

## Deposits on Banquets and Other Functions

Deposits made by customers to apply on future sales should be credited to a separate account on the books and shown as a current liability which will be offset when the customer is served.

## Income Tax—State and Federal

Estimated federal and state income taxes should be reported as a separate item in the current liability section. This total includes the unpaid income taxes for the current year and for any preceding periods.

Income taxes are a cost of doing business; consequently, they should be estimated monthly and adjusted at the end of the year.

## Current Portion of Long-Term Debt

The total of current liabilities includes all obligations due within one year. Consequently, the principal payments due the next year on any mortgage, loan or conditional sales contract are described and shown separately on the balance sheet under this heading. This division does not necessarily require a separate account on the books for these current payments if they can simply be segregated on the balance sheet. Refer to the paragraph, "Long-Term Debt," below.

## Dividends Declared and Payable

Any dividends that have been declared by the Board of Directors of a restaurant corporation and that are unpaid at the balance sheet date should be set up in a separate account and included with the current liabilities on the balance sheet.

## Total Current Liabilities

The total of current liabilities should be shown on the balance sheet so that the operator will know what the short-term cash requirements are. The operator can determine whether alternative actions are necessary to meet current obligations by comparing this total with the total of current assets and calculating the current position. Due to the fact that a restaurant typically collects receipts (cash or credit card) more quickly than it is required to pay its bills, it is very common for a restaurant's current liabilities to exceed its current assets. A more accurate picture of cash flow from the restaurant can be obtained from the statement of cash flows, discussed later in this chapter.

## Due to Officers, Stockholders, Partners

Loans and other amounts due to officers, stockholders and partners that are not to be considered a part of equity capital and are not due within one year of the balance sheet date or that are otherwise considered to be noncurrent should be shown as separate items below the total of current liabilities in the balance sheet. The repayment terms, interest rates and other pertinent information should be disclosed in the footnotes.

## Due to Affiliated or Associated Companies

The same treatment should be given to amounts payable to affiliated or associated companies as is suggested for the amounts due to officers, stockholders and partners.

## Long-Term Debt

All debt with maturities extending beyond one year of the balance sheet date should be included in this caption. Any portion of these long-term loans due within one year should be deducted from the total of the loan outstanding and shown as a current liability as explained under "Current Portion of Long-Term Debt." The calculation of the current portion is made for financial statement purposes and does not necessarily require any entries on the books of the restaurant. The repayment terms, interest rates, collateral, restrictions and other pertinent information regarding each debt should be disclosed in the footnotes along with a table setting forth the maturities of all long-term debt for the next five years.

## Deferred Income Taxes

The tax effect of temporary differences in the reporting of such items as depreciation, interest and pre-opening expenses for financial statement and tax purposes is included here.

## Other Non-Current Liabilities

Other amounts owed by the company that are not currently due and are not material may be shown under this caption. Separate captions should be used for material liabilities. Such items may include certain pension and employee benefit plans. Companies with significant pension or employee benefit plans or long term leases should consult with their accountant to determine that the liability has been calculated and reported properly.

## Capital Stock (if a Corporation)

Each class or type of capital stock should be shown separately in this section of the balance sheet. The number of shares authorized, issued and outstanding and the par or stated capital per share of stock should be indicated.

If the corporation should purchase some of its shares and hold them in its treasury for sale or re-issue, these shares should be shown as treasury stock and their cost deducted from the total capital at the bottom of the capital section of the balance sheet.

## Retained Earnings

The amount of income kept and used in the business is usually called retained earnings. A separate account should be used to accumulate these net earnings which have not been distributed to the shareholders and are thus a part of the equity capital invested in the business. The changes in the retained earnings account may be shown on the face of the statement of income if there are no changes in other capital accounts; if there are changes in other capital accounts, a separate statement reporting all changes in each equity account should be presented. A separate statement or schedule of changes in retained earnings may be presented as follows:

Retained Earnings at the Beginning of the Year      $ _____
Add: Net Income Per Statement of Income Total      _____
Deduct: Dividends (date payable)      _____
**Retained Earnings at End of Year**      $ _____

# The Statement of Income and Retained Earnings

The income statement presentation under the *Uniform System of Accounts for Restaurants* is flexible and can be readily adapted for the very small restaurant as well as for the large operation or chain. The extent to which the statement shows the detail of sales and expenses depends entirely upon the desires of the operator. A statement of income should, however, be sufficiently comprehensive to answer the questions that would normally arise in the conduct of the business.

For this reason, the various elements of operation are summarized into their major logical groupings for the preparation of the basic statement, which may be amplified indefinitely.

Although an attempt has been made in this text to list as fully as possible the items that will come under each main heading, there will always be, in the practical application of the system, some types of income or expense that are not specifically mentioned. In such cases, unlisted items should be entered in the group that contains transactions similar in nature.

In some of the larger restaurants and in chain operations, the statement presentation may be complicated by the existence of a central commissary, bakery or executive office. In these instances, the apportionment of the costs of these central units to the restaurants involved is usually made by a method or formula which best suits those in charge of operations, and their bookkeeping is designed on this particular basis. It would thus be difficult, if not impossible, to devise any uniform method of distribution for these central units that would satisfy all, since many of the distributions depend on the experience and judgment of the individual official in charge. No attempt has been made in this text to present any classifications for these central units, and the Uniform System as outlined provides only for the ultimate distribution of their costs to the retail operation of the restaurants themselves. Instead, in the Uniform System presentation, costs which occur at an executive office or commissary, and which are not allocated, are summarized in the category corporate overhead.

The form of the statement of income outlined in this section is recommended as a standard for the restaurant business. The text immediately following explains the reasoning used in arriving at this form, which is the result of the original intention to devise some uniform classification that would suit the needs of restaurants in general. Later in this chapter, the revenue and expense accounts are described in more detail, and the standard supporting schedules are illustrated.

Exhibit B

# Statement of Income and Retained Earnings
# Name of Restaurant Company
# for the Period Ended (Insert Date)

|  | Amounts | Percentages |
|---|---|---|
| **Sales** | | |
| Food | $697,000 | 82% |
| Beverage | 153,000 | 18 |
| Total Sales | 850,000 | 100 |
| | | |
| **Cost of Sales** | | |
| Food | 245,500 | 35 |
| Beverage | 52,000 | 34 |
| Total Cost of Sales | 297,500 | 35 |
| | | |
| **Gross Profit** | | |
| Food | 451,500 | 65 |
| Beverage | 101,000 | 66 |
| Total Gross Profit | 552,500 | 65 |
| | | |
| **Operating Expenses** | | |
| Salaries and Wages | 255,000 | 30 |
| Employee Benefits | 34,000 | 4 |
| Occupancy Costs | 59,200 | 7 |
| Direct Operating Expenses | 51,000 | 6 |
| Music and Entertainment | 1,000 | 00.1 |
| Marketing | 17,000 | 2 |
| Utility Services | 25,500 | 3 |
| Depreciation | 16,500 | 2 |
| General and Administrative Expenses | 44,200 | 5 |
| Repairs and Maintenance | 16,500 | 2 |
| Other Income | (2,500) | ( 00.3) |
| Total Operating Expenses | 517,400 | 61 |
| | | |
| Operating Income | 35,100 | 4 |
| Interest | 4,250 | 00.5 |
| Income Before Income taxes | 30,850 | 4 |
| Income Taxes | 4,500 | 00.5 |
| Net Income | 26,350 | 3% |
| Retained Earnings, Beginning of the Period | 175,450 | |
| Less Dividends | (10,000) | |
| **Retained Earnings, End of Period** | **$191,800** | |

Note: Numbers used are for illustrative purposes only.

## Sales

The basic element that all restaurant operations have in common is the sale of food and beverages. All the major items of cost and expense are viewed in their relationship to these sales. For this reason, the statement of income starts with food and beverage sales.

Many restaurants generate sales and income from sources other than food and beverage. Typical sources are included under other income. Other income is not included in sales for the purpose of calculating food and beverage costs and restaurant expenses. The ratios of restaurant expenses are based on their relation to food and beverage sales only, and other income does not in any way affect the expense ratio.

## Cost of Sales

The cost of merchandise sold is included in this caption. Purchases of goods for sale are based upon specifications which are in turn based on the menu. Costs of both food and beverages should not exceed a certain specified cost level relative to the sales produced. In other words, menu pricing and ingredient purchasing should be based on pre-determined desired gross profit levels. Sound management control over these two elements is necessary in any successful operation.

## Operating Expenses

Operating expenses most directly influenced by operating policy and management efficiency are listed under this major caption. They are divided into the groups or classes under which operating costs can best be summarized for the purpose of comparison, as shown in Exhibit B.

In general, all of the operating expenses of a restaurant fall into one of these categories, and this major summary classification can be used for any restaurant, large or small. Most of the major categories can also be used to advantage by such foodservice operations as department stores, inplant feeding, schools and colleges, hospitals and government and charitable institutions.

While the simplest form of statement may combine certain of these operating expeneses, the smaller operator should, in order to provide better control, divide these expenses into the major classifications shown in Exhibit B.

Salaries and wages incurred are included under one major heading. This figure includes service, preparation and administration departments.

Employee benefits are a significant expense to the restaurant operation. They include all costs directly attributable to the restaurant staff which increase in relation to the number of employees and their base salary. Employee benefits include employees' meals, federal retirement tax (FICA), federal and state unemployment tax, union and nonunion insurance premiums, state health insurance, union and nonunion pension fund contributions, workers' compensation insurance, employee relations, medical expense and other similar expenses. These expenses are included under one heading: employee benefits. This treatment is recommended in order to achieve uniformity in the operating statements.

Direct operating expenses include items such as uniforms, laundry, cleaning and other supplies, menus, replacements of linens, china, glassware, silver and utensils, and other expenses incidental to providing service to customers.

Music and entertainment costs vary widely with different types of restaurants, depending on the concept, theme, purpose and other marketing considerations. In some restaurants, entertainment consists of no more than music furnished through the restaurant sound system, operated internally. In such cases, the expense is normally included under miscellaneous expenses in direct operating expenses. Where the restaurant operator uses music and entertainment to develop business volume or to promote beverage sales with a specialty or currently popular music theme, music and entertainment costs will be a significant cost element in the operating expenses and will bring about a correspondingly marked change in other expense ratios.

The term "marketing" more accurately describes the diversified cost elements of promoting a restaurant. Advertising is only one element of marketing costs. However, some operators will prefer to retain all expenses of advertising and promotion under one heading. Others, and particularly larger restaurants, find the need to know costs relative to market research, public relations, promotion and merchandising in addition to advertising.

There is a very wide fluctuation in marketing costs depending on the policy of operation and, in many instances, on the type of patronage sought. In the statements of some of the smaller restaurants, there are few, if any, marketing expenditures; however, large restaurants and those with atmosphere or conceptual themes require a variety of marketing efforts.

Some operators may attempt to segregate utilities required in the kitchen from those incurred in the remainder of the restaurant and show the kitchen-related costs as a controllable cost. However, this process is usually difficult and, therefore, not often performed. In many leased restaurants, the expenses of water, heat and air conditioning are paid by the landlord and absorbed in the rental cost. Most restaurants group utility expenses in this one major category.

Rent, property taxes and insurance on the restaurant's premises are classified as occupancy costs. Any rent that is contingent on the restaurant reaching certain sales levels (sometimes called contingent rent or percentage rent) is also included as an occupancy cost.

The building, furniture and equipment, leasehold and leasehold improvements, which represent a large part of the investment in the business, have an economic life and will ultimately be disposed of or replaced. The costs charged against operations in the statement of income represent the pro-rated recovery cost of these items, which is called depreciation. On the balance sheet, the asset value is decreased by the amount recovered during current and prior periods.

## Interest

Interest expense is the cost of using borrowed capital. Interest on all obligations, short or long term, is included here.

## Corporate Overhead

Because corporate overhead, particularly in a chain operation, is not controllable by unit managers, it may not be allocated into the controllable expense sections of the individual restaurant's statement of income. Instead, it may be reported as a separate line item. Some companies choose to report the item only on the company's consolidated statement of income. Others allocate the expense to the individual units. The treatment of corporate overhead in the statement of income should be disclosed in the footnotes to the financial statements.

## Income Taxes

Many restaurants are operated by corporations; the income tax then becomes a part of the statement of income.

Some restaurants are operated by single proprietors or by partners who have other interests or sources of income to account for in figuring their income taxes. For this reason, their statement of income will reflect income up to but not including income taxes.

## Dividends

Amounts distributed to the holders of equity interests in the company are deducted from the total of retained earnings at the end of the prior year and the net income for the current year is added to arrive at the present balance of retained earnings. The same is true for proprietor or partners' capital.

# The Statement of Cash Flows

The balance sheet and the statement of income and retained earnings do not provide all of the financial information about an enterprise's operation. The balance sheet reflects the company's financial position as of a certain date, and the income statement shows the aggregate of revenue and expense items for a period. The missing link is a statement that shows clearly how cash generated by operating the restaurant, supplemented as necessary from other sources, was used during the period to create the financial position shown by the balance sheet. The statement of cash flows, Exhibit C, is designed to perform that function.

The statement of cash flows reports cash receipts and cash payments in three categories or activities: operating, investing and financing.

Cash flows from operating activities are generally the cash effects of transactions that involve the production and delivery of goods and services and consequently enter into the determination of net income, as well as all other transactions that are not defined as investing or financing activities.

Cash inflows from operating activities include cash receipts from the sale of goods and services and all other cash receipts that do not stem from transactions defined as investing or financing activities, such as amounts received to settle lawsuits, proceeds from insurance settlements or refunds from suppliers.

Cash outflows from operating activities include cash payments to acquire goods for resale, to employees for services, to governments for taxes, duties, fines and other fees or penalties, to lenders and other creditors for interest, and all other cash payments that do not stem from transactions defined as investing or financing activities, such as payments to settle lawsuits, cash contributions to charities and cash refunds to customers.

Investing activities include making and collecting loans and acquiring and disposing of equity investments and fixed assets. Fixed assets include assets used in restaurant operations other than items that are part of the company's inventory, such as land, buildings, leasehold improvements, furniture, fixtures and equipment.

Cash inflows from investing activities include cash receipts from collection or sale of loans made by the company and other debt instruments purchased by the company, cash receipts from sales of investments in other enterprises and cash receipts from the sale of fixed assets.

Cash outflows for investing activities include disbursements for loans made by the company and cash payments to acquire debt instruments of other entities, cash payments to acquire equity instruments of other enterprises and cash payments at the time of purchase or soon before or after purchase to acquire fixed assets.

Financing activities include the receipt of resources from owners and payments to them for a return on, and a return of, their investment, borrowing money and repaying amounts borrowed excluding interest (as payment of interest is an operating activity), and other receipts and repayments of long-term obligations.

Cash inflows from financing activities include capital contributions and the proceeds from issuing stock and proceeds from issuing bonds, mortgages, notes and other borrowings.

Cash outflows for financing activities include payments of dividends or other disbursements to owners, including outlays to re-acquire the company's equity instruments, repayments of amounts borrowed (principal only) and other principal payments to creditors who have extended long-term credit for the purchase of fixed assets, etc.

The statement of cash flows should use descriptive terms such as cash or cash and cash equivalents rather than ambiguous terms such as funds. Cash equivalents are short-term, highly-liquid investments that are both readily convertible to known amounts of cash and have maturity dates at the date of their acquisition of three months or less so that their values are determinable. Total amounts of cash and cash equivalents at the beginning and end of the period shown in the statement of cash flows should be the same amounts as similarly titled line items or subtotals shown in the balance sheet as of those dates.

Information about all investing and financing activities of the company during a period that affect recognized assets and liabilities, but not cash receipts or cash disbursements in the same period, need to be reported as well. These types of transactions are disclosed either in a narrative or summarized in a schedule, but the noncash portion of the transactions is excluded from the amounts incorporated in the statement of cash flows since they do not generate receipts or disbursements of cash. The disclosures should clearly relate the cash and noncash portions of such transactions. Examples of noncash investing and financing transactions are converting debt to equity; acquiring assets by assuming directly related liabilities, such as purchasing a building by incurring a mortgage to the seller; obtaining an asset by entering into a capital lease; and exchanging noncash assets or liabilities for other noncash assets or liabilities.

There are two methods on which the statement of cash flows can be prepared, the direct and indirect method. The direct method shows as its principal components operating cash receipts and payments, such as cash received from customers and cash paid to suppliers and employees, the sum of which is net cash flow from operating activities. The indirect method starts with net income and adjusts it for revenue and expense items that were not the result of operating cash transactions in the current period to reconcile to net cash flow from operating activities. Examples of these include depreciation and amortization expense and the deferred portion of income tax expense. Both methods are acceptable; the direct method provides additional information on operating cash receipts and disbursements, while the indirect method is easier to prepare.

Exhibit C

# Statement of Cash Flows
# Name of Restaurant Company
# Description of Period Covered by Statement
# (Direct Method)

| | |
|---|---:|
| CASH FLOWS FROM OPERATING ACTIVITIES: | |
| Cash received from customers | $ 900,000 |
| Cash paid to suppliers and employees | (845,000) |
| Interest paid (net of amount capitalized) | (2,000) |
| Income taxes paid | (1,000) |
| Insurance proceeds received | 2,350 |
| | |
| Net Cash Provided by Operating Activities | 54,350 |
| | |
| CASH FLOWS FROM INVESTING ACTIVITIES: | |
| Proceeds from sale of equipment | 1,000 |
| Cash payments for leasehold improvements | (10,000) |
| Down payment on equipment purchase | (3,000) |
| | |
| Net Cash Used in Investing Activities | (12,000) |
| | |
| CASH FLOWS FROM FINANCING ACTIVITIES: | |
| Net borrowings under line-of-credit agreement | 15,000 |
| Proceeds from issuance of long-term debt | 10,000 |
| Dividends paid | (5,000) |
| | |
| Net Cash Provided by Financing Activities | 20,000 |
| | |
| Net Increase (Decrease) In Cash and Cash Equivalents | 62,350 |
| | |
| Cash and Cash Equivalents, Beginning of Period | 662,650 |
| | |
| **Cash and Cash Equivalents, End of Period** | **$ 725,000** |

Exhibit C    page 2

## Reconciliation of net income to net cash provided by operating activities:

| | | |
|---|---:|---:|
| NET INCOME | | $26,350 |
| ADJUSTMENTS TO RECONCILE NET INCOME TO NET | | |
| CASH PROVIDED BY OPERATING ACTIVITIES: | | |
| Depreciation and amortization | | $18,000 |
| Provision for doubtful accounts | | 500 |
| Loss on sale of equipment | | 500 |
| Change in assets and liabilities: | | |
| Decrease in accounts receivable | $15,000 | |
| Increase in inventory | (10,000) | |
| Increase in prepaid expenses | (1,000) | |
| Increase in accounts payable | | |
| and accrued expenses | 5,000 | |
| Increase in interest and income taxes payable | 2,000 | |
| Decrease in other liabilities | (2,000) | 9,000 |
| Total Adjustments | | 28,000 |
| **NET CASH PROVIDED BY (USED IN) OPERATING ACTIVITIES** | | **$54,350** |

**Supplemental schedule of noncash investing and financing activities**—The Company issued  xxx additional shares of common stock in exchange for the conversion of $xx,xxx of long-term debt.

**Disclosure of accounting policy (for footnotes)**—For purposes of the statements of cash flows, the Company considers all highly-liquid debt instruments purchased with a maturity of three months or less to be cash equivalents.

Note:  Numbers used are for illustrative purposes only.

Exhibit C  page 3

# Statement of Cash Flows
# Name of Restaurant or Company
# Description of Period Covered by Statement
# (Indirect Method)

| | |
|---|---:|
| CASH FLOWS FROM OPERATING ACTIVITIES: | |
| Net Income | $ 26,350 |
| Adjustments to Reconcile Net Income to Net Cash Provided | |
| by Operating Activities: | |
| Depreciation and amortization | 18,000 |
| Provision for doubtful accounts | 500 |
| Loss on sale of equipment | 500 |
| Change in assets and liabilities: | |
| Decrease in accounts receivable | 15,000 |
| Increase in inventory | (10,000) |
| Increase in prepaid expenses | (1,000) |
| Increase (decrease) in accounts payable and accrued expenses | 5,000 |
| Increase in interest and income taxes payable | 2,000 |
| Decrease in other liabilities | (2,000) |
| Total Adjustments | 28,000 |
| **Net Cash Provided by Operating Activities** | **54,350** |
| | |
| CASH FLOWS FROM INVESTING ACTIVITIES: | |
| Proceeds from sale of equipment | 1,000 |
| Cash payments for leasehold improvements | (10,000) |
| Down payment on equipment purchase | (3,000) |
| **Net Cash Used in Investing Activities** | **(12,000)** |
| | |
| CASH FLOWS FROM FINANCING ACTIVITIES: | |
| Net borrowings under line-of-credit agreement | 15,000 |
| Proceeds from issuance of long-term debt | 10,000 |
| Dividends paid | (5,000) |
| **Net Cash Provided by Financing Activities** | **20,000** |
| **Net Increase (Decrease) In Cash and Cash Equivalents** | **62,350** |
| **CASH AND CASH EQUIVALENTS, BEGINNING OF PERIOD** | **662,650** |
| **CASH AND CASH EQUIVALENTS, END OF PERIOD** | **$725,000** |

**Supplemental disclosures of cash flow information** (for indirect method only):
Cash paid during the year for:

| | |
|---|---:|
| Interest (net of amount capitalized) | $  2,000 |
| Income taxes | $  1,000 |

**Supplemental schedule of noncash investing and financing activities**—The Company issued xxx additional shares of common stock in exchange for the conversion of $xx,xxx of long-term debt.

Exhibit C  page 4

**Disclosure of accounting policy:** For purposes of the statement of cash flows, the Company considers all highly-liquid debt instruments purchased with a maturity of three months or less to be cash equivalents.

# Notes to Financial Statements

The accounting policies and practices of the company that were followed in the preparation of the balance sheet, statement of income and retained earnings, and statement of cash flows are set forth in this section.  Among the more common notes appearing with financial statements are those which disclose the treatment of the following (not necessarily in the order indicated):

( 1) history and organization
( 2) significant accounting policies
( 3) principles and basis of consolidation
( 4) changes in accounting principles or methods
( 5) inventory methods
( 6) property, plant and equipment and depreciation
( 7) details of long-term debt and assets subject to lien
( 8) leases
( 9) commitments and contingent liabilities
(10) loan-indenture requirements and restrictions
(11) pension, profit sharing and retirement plans
(12) stock option or stock purchase plans
(13) changes in shareholders' equity (if not presented in a separate statement)
(14) income taxes and deferred taxes
(15) related party transactions, and
(16) events that have occurred since the date of the balance sheet.

Notes to the financial statements assist the reader to understand and interpret the financial condition of the company and should provide adequate disclosure of all material matters and any other information required to make the statements not misleading.

# The Statement of Income's Detailed Supporting Schedules

The following statement of income and supporting schedules, together with the accompanying explanatory text, outline the *Uniform System of Accounts for Restaurants* as approved by the National Restaurant Association.

Food sales will include the sales of coffee, tea, milk and fruit juices since these are usually served as part of a meal.  Soft drinks will also be included in food sales if the cost of such beverage is charged to food cost. If there is service of liquor, beer and wine, most restaurant operators prefer to ring up soft drinks at bar locations, thus including those sales in beverage sales.

Sales taxes are added to the total customer sale and recorded separately from sales.  Sales taxes are credited to a separate liability account until paid.

If pastry or baked goods are sold at a counter and the cost can be separated from that of the meals served to patrons, it may be desirable to show these sales and costs separately in the statement of income. The same may be true of banquet sales and outside catering; both, in some instances, are a substantial source of income for a restaurant. If sufficiently large, these operations may require a separate departmental statement: the net income of these would be included with other income as in the case of the gift-sundry shop, which will be covered later in this section.

## Use of Coupons

Frequently, restaurants will offer coupons or other discount programs to attract diners. Appropriate accounting treatment requires that the sale be recorded as the net discounted price to the customer. In order for the operator to track coupon usage and its financial impact, most operators will ring up the sale or prepare the ticket using the menu price and then record a deduction for the discount as a contra to the sales account. Most electronic cash registers are designed to track coupon usage in this manner. For this reason, a separate account number for coupon usage within sales has been included in the *Uniform System of Accounts for Restaurants.*

# Summary Statement of Income
## Name of Restaurant Company
## Description of Period Covered by Statement

| | Exhibit | Amounts | Percentages |
|---|---|---|---|
| SALES: | | | |
| Food | D | $ | % |
| Beverage | E | | |
| **Total Sales** | | | |
| | | | |
| COST OF SALES: | | | |
| Food | | | |
| Beverage | | | |
| **Total Cost of Sales** | | | |
| **Gross Profit** | | | |
| | | | |
| OPERATING EXPENSES: | | | |
| Salaries and Wages | F | | |
| Employee Benefits | G | | |
| Direct Operating Expenses | H | | |
| Music and Entertainment | I | | |
| Marketing | J | | |
| Utility Services | K | | |
| General and Administrative Expenses | L | | |
| Repairs and Maintenance | M | | |
| Occupancy Costs | N | | |
| Depreciation | N | | |
| Other Income | O | | |
| **Total Operating Expenses** | | | |
| | | | |
| Operating Income | | | |
| Interest | P | | |
| Income Before Income Taxes | | | |
| Income Taxes | | | |
| **NET INCOME** | | $ | % |

# Food Sales

| | Meals Served | Amounts $ | Percentages % |
|---|---|---|---|
| BY MEAL PERIOD: | | | |
| Breakfast | | | |
| Lunch | | | |
| Dinner | _____ | _____ | _____ |
| | | | |
| **Total Dining Room** | | | |
| Banquets | _____ | | |
| **Total Meals Served** | _____ | | |
| | | | |
| Bakery | | | |
| Take-out | | | |
| Outside Catering | | _____ | _____ |
| **TOTAL FOOD SALES** | | $_____ | _____% |

| | Meals Served | Amounts | Percentages |
|---|---|---|---|
| BY LOCATIONS: | | | |
| Dining Room | | $ | % |
| Coffee Shop | | | |
| Luncheon Terrace | | | |
| Grill | | | |
| Cafeteria | | | |
| Patio | | | |
| Drive-Thru | | | |
| Take-out | | | |
| Banquets | _____ | _____ | _____ |
| | | | |
| **Total Meals Served** | _____ | | |
| | | | |
| Bakery | | | |
| Take-out | | | |
| Outside Catering | | _____ | _____ |
| **Total Food Sales** | | $_____ | _____% |

## Food and Beverage Sales

Many operators want to detail the makeup of food sales in order to accurately evaluate the kind of business being done. Divisions are often made between meal periods and source locations, such as by dining area, banquet and catering as shown in Exhibit D. This kind of information and the statistical information which follows are valuable in developing and monitoring marketing efforts.

## Food Sales Statistics

A knowledge of food sales statistics can be helpful in many ways. In addition to use in marketing, for example, statistics can indicate whether the high- and low-priced items on the menu are properly balanced and are holding popularity according to plan. The number of customers served is an important measure of acceptance. It also is the basis for the average sale per customer, which helps the operator to monitor the effect of menu-pricing policies. Statistical information used to measure the efficiency of the layout includes sales per seat and customer turnover per seat. How efficiently the employees' time is scheduled is measured by the number of meals served per waiter or waitress. An example of such statistics and a description of how they are compiled is included here.

The sales are divided by the number of customers served, and the resulting average check per customer is shown as follows:

| Meal Period | Food Sales | | Customers Served | | Average Check |
|---|---|---|---|---|---|
| Breakfast | $ 500.00 | divided by | 200 | = | $2.50 |
| Lunch | 1,200.00 | divided by | 260 | = | 4.62 |
| Dinner | 1,100.00 | divided by | 100 | = | 11.00 |
| Total | $2,800.00 | | 560 | | $5.00 |

If there were 100 seats in this restaurant, the average daily turnover per seat would be as follows:

| Meal Period | Average Daily Food Sales Per Seat | Daily Customer Turnover Per Seat |
|---|---|---|
| Breakfast | $ 5.00 | 2.00 |
| Lunch | 12.00 | 2.60 |
| Dinner | 11.00 | 1.00 |
| Total | $28.00 | 5.60 |

The customers and sales per server were calculated as follows:

| Meal Period | Number of Servers | Average Sales Per Server | Customers Served Per Server |
|---|---|---|---|
| Breakfast | 6.00 | $3.33 | 33.3 |
| Lunch | 10.00 | 120.00 | 26.0 |
| Dinner | 6.00 | 183.33 | 16.7 |
| Total | 7.33* | $386.66 | 76.0 |

(*Note: The number of servers divided by the three meal periods equals the average number of servers per day as shown on the total line.)

Certain operators have also found it practical to control salaries and wages on the basis of production, as measured by the number of persons served, of cooks and warewashers.

However, in the ordinary restaurant, the use of operating expense ratios and meal statistics should be sufficient amplification of the operating figures to give a restaurant operator a clear picture of the business. The operator can always go into greater detail when something appears to be wrong after comparison of the regular statements from one period to the next.

Exhibit E
# Beverage Sales

| BY TYPE OF DRINK: | Amounts | Percentages |
|---|---|---|
| Mixed Drinks and Cocktails | $ | % |
| Beer | | |
| Wines | | |
| Soft Drinks | | |
| Bottle Sales | _____ | _____ |
| | | |
| **Total Beverage Sales** | **$_____** | **100%** |
| | | |
| BY BAR LOCATION: | | |
| Main Bar | $ | |
| Service Bar | | |
| Dining Room | | |
| Grill | | |
| Patio | | |
| Banquets and Parties | | |
| Bottle Sales | _____ | _____ |
| | | |
| **Total Beverage Sales** | **$_____** | **100%** |

Food sales by items sold may be analyzed from customers' checks or taken from electronic, point-of-sale registers. The popularity of various foods is determined this way, and sales of high cost items, such as steaks, roast beef and lobster, can be accounted for to provide closer control. The periodic test of customers' checks against inventory of any particular item is a basic control now made very practical because of the versatility of point-of-sale devices. It is, therefore, important to record customer counts accurately whether from preset machine-generated records or from reading the customers' checks, properly filled out by the server.

Care should be taken to record the correct number of customers. If two customers are recorded but only one eats food, then the average food check would be distorted. The number of customers eating food is generally used, although some operators prefer to count both food and beverage customers, thus providing the total of all sales per customer.

The sale of beverages, which would include all alcoholic beverages and soft drinks, is shown separately on the statement of income. These sales would not include coffee, tea, milk or fruit juices, which are considered food items since they are normally served with meals. The sales tax collected from the customer is not included in the beverage sales.

Because the percentage of gross profit varies considerably for the different types of beverage sales, it may be helpful to operators to divide the beverage sales into several major groups, such as cocktails, liquors, wines, beers, non-alcoholic drinks and bottle sales as shown in Schedule F. This can be done by means of separate keys on the point-of-sale register or by a daily analysis of the beverage checks.

Beverage sales may also be summarized by meal periods or by dining rooms and types of service.

If a detailed analysis is required for an open or cash bar, it is best accomplished by an analysis of the beverage consumed through the application of a potential sales value technique. This technique is discussed later in this book.

The number of beverage customers served and the sales per customer are statistics that are available from the point-of-sale registers; however, few operators maintain this statistic. A number of operators do compute the average sale for combined food and beverage sales.

## Food Cost

The cost of food consumed is normally calculated in the following manner:

| | | |
|---|---:|---:|
| Beginning Inventory | | $ 5,000 |
| Add: | | |
|   Food Purchases | $19,000 | |
|   Delivery Charges | 200 | 19,200 |
|   Total | | 24,200 |
| Deduct: | | |
|   Ending Inventory | | 6,000 |
| **Cost of Food Consumed** | | **$18,200** |

If a general storeroom is maintained, the food purchases would be separated into food items sent directly to the kitchen for production and the food items delivered to the storeroom and later issued by requisition. In this case, a separate control on the storeroom is desirable, and the food cost calculation would probably be as follows:

## Storeroom

| | |
|---|---:|
| Beginning Inventory | $ 4,000 |
| Food Stores Purchased | 16,000 |
| | |
| Total | 20,000 |
| Issues per Requisition | 14,400 |
| | |
| Balance to Account For | 5,600 |
| Ending Inventory | 5,000 |
| | |
| **Inventory Over or (Short)** | **$ (600)** |

The food issues from the storeroom, plus or minus the inventory over or short, would become a part of the cost of food consumed, calculated as follows:

| | | |
|---|---:|---:|
| Beginning Kitchen Inventory | | $ 1,000 |
| Direct Food Purchases | $ 3,000 | |
| Storeroom (Issues and Shortages) | 15,000 | |
| Express and Delivery | 200 | 18,200 |
| | | |
| Total | | 19,200 |
| | | |
| Ending Kitchen Inventory | | 1,000 |
| | | |
| **Cost of Food Consumed** | | **$ 18,200** |

The costs of coffee, tea, milk and soda fountain supplies are to be included in food cost.

## Employees' Meals

The food cost calculations shown thus far do not take into consideration the amount of food used for employees' meals. Many of the smaller restaurants, and some of the larger ones, do not make any provision for the cost of employees' meals, and thus their food costs are called gross costs or cost of food consumed. It is for this reason that in the Uniform System the cost of employees' meals is shown as a separate item when it is calculated. The statement of income thus indicates that the food-cost figure, used in computing the gross profit, is the net cost after deducting employees meals.

Actually, the separation of the food cost between the cost of food served to guests and that served to employees is made in order to indicate more clearly the direct relation of menu prices to costs.

While there are many ways in which employees' meal costs are calculated, nearly all of them are based on food cost alone; no attempt is made to apportion payroll or other expenses of operation to this item. Of course, if a separate employees' dining room or cafeteria is maintained, it may be possible to cost the food transfers to that room and charge the direct payroll and expenses of service to these meals. However, in most instances the employees use a part of the working or dining room space and serve themselves.

Thus, in the majority of cases, the policy of each individual restaurant related to meals allowed to employees is followed in arriving at a total count of meals from the payroll record. These meals are then priced on an estimated and often arbitrary cost basis; the number of meals times this cost per meal is the total cost of employees' meals.

Where certain employees, such as executives, department heads and others, are served in the dining room, their meals are usually recorded on a special or officer's check at menu prices, and the amounts are not included with the sales to customers. In these instances the cost of employees' meals is calculated by the method shown in the following example:

| Net Food Cost—Including Officers' Checks | $ | Annual | % |
|---|---|---|---|
| Sales to Customers | | $1,000,000 | |
| Officers' Checks | | 30,000 | |
| Total, at Menu Prices | | 1,030,000 | |
| Cost of Food Consumed | | 400,000 | |
| Deduct: Cost of Employees' Meals | | | |
| Not Recorded on Check—20,000 Meals at $2.00 | | 40,000 | |
| Net Food Cost—Including Officers' Checks | | $ 360,000 | |
| Ratio of Net Cost to Total at Menu Prices— | | | |
| 360,000 divided by 1,030,000 | | | 34.95% |
| **Employees' Meals Cost** | | | |
| Officers' Checks $30,000 x 34.95% | | $ 10,500 | |
| Meals Not on Checks | | 40,000 | |
| Total Employees' Meals | | $ 50,500 | |
| **Cost of Food Sold** | | | |
| Sales to Customers | $1,000,000 | | 100.00% |
| Cost of Food Consumed | | 400,000 | |
| Deduct: Employees' Meals | | 50,500 | 5.05 |
| Cost of Food Sold | | 349,500 | 34.95 |
| Gross Profit on Food Sales | | $ 650,500 | 65.05% |

Whatever the method used, the amount calculated for employees' meals is influenced by the value placed on meals not recorded on checks. This amount can be estimated by someone familiar with the type of meals served to these employees. The cost of employee meals should be accurately determined by type of meal eaten, i.e., breakfast, lunch or dinner, for purposes of the statement of income. The cost of employees' meals is used only to determine the net cost of food sold.

## Beverage Cost

The cost of beverages is ordinarily computed as follows:

| | | |
|---|---:|---:|
| Beginning Inventory | | $ 5,000 |
| Add: | | |
|   Purchases | $4,700 | |
|   Food (Transferred from Food Cost) | 300 | |
|   Express and Delivery Charges | 100 | 5,100 |
| | | |
| Total | | 10,100 |
| Deduct Ending Inventory | | 5,100 |
| **Cost of Beverages** | | **$ 5,000** |

If a beverage storeroom is maintained, it would be advisable to control it by means of a perpetual inventory. All purchases of liquors, wines and beers would be charged to the storeroom and issued on requisition as they are needed at the bar. It is also advisable to establish a par stock for the bar, which is to be maintained by replenishing the stock each morning. In this manner, the morning requisition, plus the interim issues to the bar the day before, will approximate the beverage cost for that day, which can be compared with the sales for daily control purposes.

In this case a separate control is kept on the storeroom stock, and the beverage cost would be figured as follows:

| | |
|---|---:|
| STOREROOM: | |
| Beginning Inventory | $ 3,000 |
| Purchases | 4,700 |
|   Total | 7,700 |
| Issues to Bar | (4,200) |
|   Balance | 3,500 |
|   Ending Inventory | 3,400 |
| **Inventory Over or (Short)** | **$ (100)** |

Thus, the issues to the bar, plus the storeroom shortage or minus the storeroom overage, would become a part of the cost of beverages calculated as follows:

| | | |
|---|---:|---:|
| Beginning Bar Stock | | $ 1,400 |
| Add: | | |
|   Storeroom Issues | $4,300 | |
|   Bar Groceries | 300 | |
|   Express and Cartage | 100 | 4,700 |
| | | |
| Total | | 6,100 |
| | | |
| Deduct: | | |
|   Ending Bar Stock | | 1,100 |
| **Cost of Beverages** | | **$5,000** |

An inventory of each bar should be taken at least once a month after the close of business on the last day of the month or of the accounting period. In many instances, bar inventory is taken once in the middle of the month and again on the last day. Some operators take the bar inventories weekly. The frequency of bar inventory taking is often a reflection of the need to control costs when these costs do not reach expectations or potential.

The bar inventory amount will fluctuate, depending on how accurately it is replenished from the storeroom stock each day and how accurately it is taken, for there will always be partially filled bottles to be considered. Many operators believe that the most accurate and the most practical method of calculating the part bottles is by counting in tenths.

The inventory values will fluctuate slightly even if a par stock is maintained because of the partially filled bottles, changes in cost prices, and the shortages and overages in the inventory count. These fluctuations in bar inventory will add or subtract from the beverage cost. For instance, in the calculations used as an illustration, the storeroom inventory showed a shortage of $100; and the bar inventory went down $300.

When pricing inventories, the average current invoiced price should be used in most instances since turnover is frequent enough not to distort the value. However, in restaurants where certain stocks move more slowly or when large quantity purchases are made, the operator should use prices applicable to those purchases.

In some states, the beverage supplier will discount an invoice by reducing the cost price of certain types by a percentage of cost per case. The amount of discount should be credited to other income. The per bottle cost should not be reduced by the amount of the discount.

Some states allow purveyors to provide discounts on alcoholic beverages by supplying extra bottles. When that happens, the cost per bottle is computed as follows:

| | |
|---|---:|
| 24 bottles (2 cases) of brand "X" @ $10.00 | $240.00 |
| 2 bottles of brand "X" @; no charge | NC |
| Total 26 bottles at $9.23 | $240.00 |

The cost per bottle is $240.00 divided by 26 bottles or $9.23

The bottles purchased with extra bottle discounts should be inventoried and issued at prices calculated as shown. The storeroom may contain prior purchases of several additional cases of brand "X," but these should be priced at the invoiced price.

## Salaries and Wages

Under the Uniform System, salaries and wages are included under one major group. This amount includes the regular salaries and wages, extra wages, overtime, vacation pay and any commission or bonus payments to employees.

In the case of single proprietors and partnerships, the payment to the owners in recognition of their management is part of net income and does not appear as part of the payroll. In some circumstances, administrative salaries might include officers' salaries that could, under other circumstances, be deemed disproportionately high. It could be feasible and practical in individual instances to arrive at a management and administrative salary that would be comparable with that paid a hired manager performing the same services. It is well, however, to keep this matter of proprietors' or partners' salaries in mind when making comparisons of the individual restaurant with others under the Uniform System.

If it seems desirable, a sub-classification can be made of the salaries and wages by dividing it into major groups, such as service, preparation, warewashing, storeroom, clerical and administrative. It may also be desirable to further divide the payroll according to the various dining areas served, such as main dining room, coffee shop, cafeteria, bar, banquets and parties.

Exhibit F is a suggested detailed distribution, showing the number of employees in the regular payroll, their regular pay and the amount of extra wages. Not all accounts listed will apply to all restaurants.

## Service Charge Distribution

Service charges may or may not be distributed to employees. In the Uniform System, service charges are included in other income.

Some restaurants distribute the entire service charge (usually associated with banquets or large parties), while others distribute only a portion. In order not to alter the relationship of food and beverage sales to related costs, the excess net service charge should be included as other income in the statement of income.

As service charges are made in lieu of tips, they are generally not considered a part of sales for state and local tax purposes. Any service charges not distributed to employees are included as other income.

Exhibit F
# Salaries and Wages

| | Number of Employees | Amounts | |
| --- | --- | --- | --- |
| | | Regular Payroll | Extra Wages |
| **SERVICE:** | | | |
| Head Waitstaff, Chief Hostess | | $ | $ |
| Captains, Hostesses, Receptionists | | | |
| Waiters, Waitresses | | | |
| Counter Service (Cafeteria) | | | |
| Buspersons, Runners | | | |
| Banquet or Extra Waiters, Waitresses | | | |
| Cashiers and Checkers | | | |
| Order Clerks (Bakery or Takeout Counter) | ____ | ____ | ____ |
| **Total Service** | ____ | ____ | ____ |
| | | | |
| **BEVERAGES:** | | | |
| Wine Steward, Storeroom Attendants | | | |
| Bartenders | | | |
| Bar Porters | | | |
| Beverage Controller and Bar Cashiers | ____ | ____ | ____ |
| **Total Beverages** | ____ | ____ | ____ |
| | | | |
| **PREPARATION:** | | | |
| Chef, Head Dietitian, Kitchen Manager | | | |
| Cooks | | | |
| Short Order Cooks | | | |
| Fountain Attendants | | | |
| Pantry and Salads | | | |
| Butcher Shop, Bake Shop, Pastry | | | |
| Coffee Attendant | | | |
| Potwashers | | | |
| Vegetable Cleaners | | | |
| Runners | | | |
| Steward and Assistants | ____ | ____ | ____ |
| **Total Preparation** | ____ | ____ | ____ |
| | | | |
| **SANITATION:** | | | |
| Warewashers | | | |
| Porters | | | |
| Cleaners | | | |
| **Total Sanitation** | ____ | ____ | ____ |
| | ____ | ____ | ____ |
| **PURCHASING AND STORING:** | | | |
| Purchasing Steward | | | |
| Receiving Clerk | | | |
| Storeroom | | | |
| Food Controller | | | |
| **Total Purchasing and Storing** | ____ | ____ | ____ |
| | ____ | ____ | ____ |

| | Number of Employees | Amounts | |
|---|---|---|---|
| | | **Regular Payroll** | **Extra Wages** |
| ADMINISTRATIVE: | | | |
| Administrative and Officers' Salaries | | $ | $ |
| Manager | | | |
| Manager's Office | | | |
| Banquet Sales Office | | | |
| Outside Catering | | | |
| Accounting Office | | | |
| Personnel and Payroll Office | | | |
| Data Processing | | | |
| Telephone Operators | | | |
| Security Personnel | ____ | ____ | ____ |
| **Total Administrative** | ____ | ____ | ____ |
| | | | |
| OTHER: | | | |
| Engineers | | | |
| Maintenance Staff | | | |
| Gardeners | | | |
| Door Attendants | | | |
| Parking Lot Attendants | | | |
| Gift and Sundry Shop Staff | ____ | ____ | ____ |
| **Total Other** | ____ | ____ | ____ |
| **TOTAL SALARIES AND WAGES** | ____ | $____ | $____ |

## Employee Benefits

Exhibit G demonstrates the categorization of employee benefit expenses under the Uniform System. These accounts are self-explanatory; not all restaurants will have these expenses.

The calculation and treatment of employees' meals in the statement of income under the Uniform System have been described in detail earlier in this text in connection with food cost. Although shown as a separate expense on some statements of income, the expense is an employee benefit and as such should logically be included here.

Many small restaurant operators, and some larger ones, make no calculation of the cost of employees' meals; in these cases, the gross food cost or cost of food consumed is shown in the statement of income.

Some restaurant operators are charging employees for their meals (at discount prices) and increasing cash wages accordingly. This policy makes unnecessary the calculation of reasonable cost and the consideration of menu restrictions for employees. It is also considered by some operators as providing a tighter control, which results in savings on employees' meal cost.

# Employee Benefits

| | Amounts |
|---|---|
| PAYROLL TAXES: | |
| Federal Retirement Tax (FICA) | $ |
| Federal Unemployment Tax | |
| State Unemployment Tax | |
| State Health Insurance Tax | |
| Other Payroll Taxes | |
| **Total Payroll Taxes** | ———— |
| | ———— |
| INSURANCE: | |
| Worker's Compensation Insurance Premiums | |
| Welfare Plan Payments | |
| Pension Plan Payments | |
| Accident and Health Insurance Premiums | |
| Hospitalization, Group Insurance Premiums | |
| **Total Insurance** | ———— |
| | ———— |
| EMPLOYEES MEALS | ———— |
| OTHER EXPENSES: | |
| Employee Instruction and Education Expenses | |
| Employee Christmas and Other Parties | |
| Employee Sports Activities | |
| Medical Expenses | |
| Credit Union | |
| Awards and Prizes | |
| Transportation and Housing | |
| **Total Other Expenses** | ———— |
| | ———— |
| **TOTAL EMPLOYEE BENEFITS** | $———— |

## Prime Cost

The term prime cost is sometimes used to denote the combination of the cost of food sold and preparation or kitchen labor. Those combined costs may range from 45 to 50% of food sales, depending upon the type of restaurant and many other factors. Operators consider the measurement useful for setting menu prices. Where there is not sufficient information available upon which to measure preparation labor, the total cost of food and beverages sold and salaries and wages can be used as a base. These combined costs generally comprise 60% to 70% of sales in restaurant operations, depending upon the type of menu and other factors.

Exhibit H
# Direct Operating Expenses

Uniforms
Laundry and Dry Cleaning
Linen Rental
Tableware and Linen
Kitchen Utensils
Supplies
Menus and Drink Lists
Contract Cleaning
Flowers and Decorations
Auto or Truck Expenses
Employee Transportation
Freight
Licenses and Permits
Banquet Expenses
Miscellaneous                                                                    _____

**TOTAL DIRECT OPERATING EXPENSES**                                        $_____

## Direct Operating Expenses

The various items that are indicated under this major heading demand more than just a listing to describe them properly and give the reasons for their inclusion. For the most part, they are expenses directly involved in the service to the customer, which is why they are described as direct expenses. An attempt is made, insofar as possible, to list the closely related expenses next to each other. They then might be combined in the statement of income if the restaurant operator does not need as extensive a listing of accounts as is shown in Exhibit H.   At the same time, it should be noted from some of the detailed descriptions that it is possible to divide the items into even greater detail than is shown by the accounts listed, if desired.

### Uniforms

This amount includes the cost of all uniforms purchased, cleaning and repairing them, and badges. Some of the items included under uniform expense are:

aprons                          ties
blouses                         trousers
caps                            shirtfronts
coats                           hairnets
dresses                         shoes
smocks                          costumes
gloves                          badges
suits

## Laundry and Dry Cleaning

This category includes the cost of laundering table linens and uniforms, napkin, towel and apron service, and cleaning uniforms, wall and window hangings, and floor coverings.

## Linen Rental

If the linen is not owned by the restaurant but is rented, such rental service cost is shown in this account; or it may, for convenience, be included with the laundry cost, as linen and laundry services are often related and supplied by the same company.

## Replacement of Linen, China, Glassware, Silver, Utensils

Most restaurant operators consider the replacement costs of linens, china, glassware, silver and utensils as a direct service cost rather than as a repair and maintenance item, and for this reason these replacements are included in the direct operating expense group.

In the small restaurant, the cost of these replacements is usually charged to expense when the purchase is recorded and very often all of these costs are grouped into one account. However, since these replacement purchases are often made in quantities that would distort the expense ratios in the month in which they are purchased, a more equitable method would be to make monthly charges equal to a pro-rata share of maintaining this equipment at a practical level. The charges would be based on a ratio to food and beverage sales which has been indicated by past experience or by comparison with the averages for other restaurants. The amount of these estimated charges to expense is credited to a reserve account, and the cost of the actual replacements is charged against this reserve. At the close of the year, this reserve can be adjusted to equal the purchases for that year if no inventories are taken of this equipment or to the amounts actually used up if the equipment is controlled by means of inventories.

As a practical matter, inventories are not usually taken on this type of equipment. Rather these expenses are based on the actual purchases, and the inventories' fluctuations are disregarded. These inventory methods are mentioned for the benefit of those who desire a more accurate statement of these costs.

## Tableware and Linen

Items included in this group are:

LINEN:
napkins
tablecloths
doilies

table tops
table protectors
side towels

TABLEWARE:
plates
cups
saucers
bowls
compotes
coffee and teapots
platters

pitchers
drinking glasses
goblets
wine glasses
shot glasses
tumblers
cordial glasses

SILVERWARE:
flatware
hollowware
ladles
serving dishes
candelabra

ice cream dishes
bowls
platters
trays
decorative pieces

Disposable service would also be included under this caption.

## Kitchen Utensils

This account includes the cost of replacing tools and small equipment used in the kitchen and the cost of their repair, including knife sharpening, soldering, etc.

The items in this group are:

knives                              mixing bowls
cleavers and other tools            beaters
pots                                skewers
pans                                mixing spoons
kettles                             can openers

Bar utensils are not included here as they are listed as a bar expense.

## Supplies

In the case of most restaurants, this group of expenses should be put in one account; in the larger operations, however, they may be divided into cleaning supplies, paper supplies, guest supplies and bar supplies.

Items to be included here are suggested by the following:

CLEANING SUPPLIES:
cleaning fluids                     brooms and sweepers
cleaning compounds                  mops
polish                              brushes
soaps                               cleaning cloths
detergents                          dust cloths
disinfectants                       pails
cleaning chemicals                  rags
deodorants                          steel wool

PAPER SUPPLIES:
cups                                soufflé cups
doilies                             holders
liners                              pastry bags
napkins                             filter paper
plates                              wax paper
wrapping paper                      twine
boxes

GUEST SUPPLIES:
matches                             toothpicks
favors and small gifts              score pads for cards
newspapers                          prizes
souvenirs                           postal cards

BAR SUPPLIES:
corkscrews                          measuring rules
mixers                              knives
bottle openers                      strainers
shakers                             bottle stoppers
spoons                              swizzle sticks
fruit squeezers                     toothpicks
fancy drink decorations             gratis food (such as
favors and small gifts                  nuts, popcorn, chips)
souvenirs

## Menus and Drink Lists

The cost of art work, cuts, paper stock, and the printing of menus and beverage lists, whether they are purchased from the outside or prepared by the restaurant personnel, should be included in this category. Where the cost is too small to warrant separation, this expense might be combined with printing and stationery expense under the general heading of administrative and general expenses, detailed in a later paragraph.

## Contract Cleaning

The cost of service contracts for night cleaning, window washing, extermination and disinfecting should be charged to this account.

## Flowers and Decorations

Items to be included in this account are the cost of cut flowers, ferns, palms, artificial flowers, plants, flags, bunting, decorative pieces prepared for tables or display, song birds, goldfish, etc., used for table or dining room decorations. It will also include the cost of the services of any florist, window dresser or similar specialist. The cost of special holiday decorations would also be charged to this account. Ice carvings used as table decorations or display should also be charged here.

If special decorations or flowers are purchased for banquets and parties and the customer is charged for them separately from the cost of the meal, this cost should be offset against the income which would be shown under other income.

## Auto or Truck Expense

Some restaurants maintain their own automobile or truck for the transportation of food and supplies from the market or for delivery purposes in the case of outside catering. This account should be charged with the cost of gasoline, oil, licenses and repairs for these vehicles. If a car rental or delivery service contract is used, the cost should also be included here.

## Freight

Although it is advisable to charge freight costs in connection with food and beverage purchases to the food and beverage cost, these expenses are often shown in the expense section of the statement of income. Therefore, if this is found to be a more practical procedure, these expenses should be included in this direct operating expense category.

## Parking

Parking space for customers' automobiles is vital to most restaurants. Any parking lot rental, garage or other costs in connection with the parking of customers' cars should be included in this account.

## Licenses and Permits

This account should be charged with all federal, state and municipal licenses in connection with the restaurant, bar, food or cabaret operations. The cost of special permits and inspection fees should also be included here.

No sales, franchise or other taxes, however, are to be charged to this account as they are provided for elsewhere in the statement of income.

## Banquet Expense

Included in this account are expenses incurred in connection with banquet and party service which cannot properly be included in other expense groups already listed. Such items would be chair or equipment rental, party favors and special decorations.

## Miscellaneous

This classification is to include all items attributable directly to the service of the customer that cannot be classified under previous headings, such as the cost of laboratory tests, lost and damaged articles and snow shoveling.

Exhibit I

# Music and Entertainment

|  | **Amounts** |
|---|---|
| Orchestras and Musicians | $ |
| Professional Entertainers | |
| Mechanical Music | |
| Contracted Wire Services | |
| Piano Rental and Tuning | |
| Films, Records, Sheet Music | |
| Programs | |
| Booking Agent's Fees | |
| Meals Served to Musicians and Entertainers | _____ |
| **TOTAL MUSIC AND ENTERTAINMENT** | $_____ |

## Music and Entertainment

The items in Exhibit I are self-explanatory and fully descriptive of the costs and expenses to be charged to this account and are not discussed in further detail.

Exhibit J

# Marketing

Selling and Promotion      $
Advertising
Public Relations and Publicity
Fees and Commissions
Research                 _____

**TOTAL MARKETING**       $_____

# Marketing

There are several activities that are necessary to make the public aware of the restaurant, the type of food and drink served, the level of service and the atmosphere. These activities are interdependent and make up the costs grouped together in marketing. The expense categories associated with the marketing effort are listed in Exhibit J. When combined, they show the results of using all of the techniques of public relations, selling, merchandising and promotion, both by outside agencies and also the restaurant staff.

Items to be included in the five marketing categories are suggested as follows:

SELLING AND PROMOTION:

    Sales representative service
    Travel expense on solicitation
    Direct mail
    Entertainment costs in promotion of business (including gratis meals to customers)
    Postage

ADVERTISING:

    Newspapers
    Magazines and trade journals
    Circulars, brochures, postal cards and other mailing pieces
    Outdoor signs
    Radio and television
    Programs, directories and guides
    Preparation of copy, photographs, etc.

PUBLIC RELATIONS AND PUBLICITY:

    Civic and community projects
    Donations (may be cash, food, gift certificates)
    Souvenirs, favors, treasure chest items
    Sports team sponsorship

FEES AND COMMISSIONS:

    Advertising or promotional agency fees

RESEARCH:

    Travel in connection with research
    Outside research agency
    Product testing

## Utility Services

The expenses associated with utility services are listed in Exhibit K.

### Electric Current

The cost of electricity purchased is charged to this account. The cost of repair service should also be charged to this account.

Exhibit K

# Utility Services

|  | Amounts |
|---|---|
| Electric Current | $ |
| Electric Bulbs | |
| Fuel | |
| Water | |
| Ice and Refrigeration Supplies | |
| Removal of Waste | |
| Engineer's Supplies | |
| **Total Energy and Utility Services** | $_____ |
| Deduct: | |
| Recycling Credits | |
| Sales to Tenants | |
| **Net Cost to Restaurant** | $_____ |

### Fuel

This account should include the cost of all fuel, including oil or gas.

In some instances where the restaurant is on rented property, the rental charge might include certain utilities. Restaurant operators who pay for their own heat and water group these costs with the other utility costs of the restaurant.

### Water

This account is charged with the cost of water consumed and with any chemicals, such as water softener or purifying compounds used.

### Ice and Refrigeration Supplies

The cost of supplies for the ice machines should be charged here.

Ice purchased to be used for ice carvings for table or banquet decorations should be charged to direct operating expenses under the caption, flowers and decorations.

Some restaurant operators believe that ice used for table and bar service should also be considered a direct operating expense rather than a utility cost. In a uniform statement presentation, it is more logical to charge all refrigeration and ice production costs in one account as a utility item.

### Removal of Waste

This account will be charged with the cost of garbage disposal and of the removal of rubbish and waste matter, usually done under contract. Any incinerator expense would also be included here.

### Engineer's Supplies

The cost of oils, boiler compound, fuses, grease, solvents, packing and other supplies, plus any small tools used in the operation or maintenance of the mechanical and electrical equipment, should be charged to this account.

### Recycling Credits

Any waste or other items recycled for cash should be treated as a reduction in utility services and credited to these expenses here.

### Sales to Tenants

In the event that the restaurant has income from the sale of electricity, ice, water or other utility items to a tenant, subtenant or concessionaire, these sales should be regarded as a reduction in the utility costs of the restaurant and should be credited to this group of expenses.

Exhibit L

# General and Administrative Expenses

| | Amounts |
|---|---|
| Office Stationery, Printing and Supplies | $ |
| Postage | |
| Telephone | |
| Data Processing Costs | |
| Directors' or Trustees' Fees | |
| Dues and Subscriptions | |
| Traveling Expenses | |
| Insurance - General | |
| Commission on Credit Card Charges | |
| Collection Fees | |
| Provision for Doubtful Accounts | |
| Cash Shortages | |
| Claims and Damages Paid | |
| Professional Fees | |
| Protective Services | |
| Bank Deposit Pickup Services | |
| Sales Taxes | |
| Training Costs | |
| Personnel Expense | |
| Corporate Overhead | |
| Miscellaneous | |
| **Total General and Administrative Expenses** | $_____ |

## General and Administrative Expenses

This group of expenses, listed in Exhibit L, is commonly considered as overhead, and the items included here are those necessary to the operation of the business rather than those connected directly with the service and comfort of the customer.

### Office Stationery, Printing and Supplies

This account should be charged with the cost of all printed matter not devoted to advertising and promotion, such as accounting forms, account books, restaurant checks, office supplies, cash register and other checking supplies, letterheads, bills and envelopes.

## Postage

All postage except amounts applicable to advertising should be charged here.

## Telephone

The cost of telephone equipment rental and local and long distance calls should be charged to this account with the exception of calls chargeable to marketing. Instances where paging equipment, internal telephone system, or cellular phones are used, the costs of related service and supplies may also be charged to this account.

## Data Processing Costs

The cost of electronic data processing and the accompanying amortization of software costs are charged to this account. The expense of outside computer services, such as preparation of payroll, is also included. Fees paid to banks or other organizations to process information should be entered under this heading. Depreciation of owned EDP equipment is included with other depreciation.

## Directors' and Trustees' Fees

The fees and expenses of directors, trustees, registrars or others in like capacity should be charged to this account.

## Dues and Subscriptions

The dues paid for membership in trade or business organizations or for authorized members of the staff to represent the restaurant in such associations are charged to this account. The cost of subscriptions to trade journals and magazines used by the management or staff should also be included here.

## Traveling Expense

The cost of the maintenance and transportation of the manager or staff members of the restaurant when they are traveling on business is to be charged to this account in all cases except when traveling is done in connection with business promotion. In those cases, the expense is charged to marketing under the heading of selling and promotion.

## Insurance—General

All types of insurance costs, other than those included as employee benefits or fire and extended coverage on the premises and contents, should be charged to this account. The types of insurance costs included here are:

burglary, holdup, forgery, fraud, robbery
fidelity bonds
public, boiler and elevator liability
use and occupancy
partners' or officers' life insurance

## Commission on Credit Card Charges

The fee charged by credit card organizations for central billing and collection of credit card accounts is charged here.

## Collection Fees

This account is charged with the cost of collecting customers' accounts, collection agency, attorneys' and notary fees, and the cost of credit reports.

## Provision for Doubtful Accounts

A charge sufficient to provide for the probable loss in collection of customer accounts, returned checks and other receivables should be charged to this account, with an accompanying credit to the allowance for doubtful accounts. If this method is used, any accounts written off will be charged against the allowance account. If this method is not used, any accounts written off should be charged directly to this account.

## Cash Shortages

Cashiers' shortages not recovered should be charged to this account. If there is a cash overage, the account should be credited.

## Claims and Damages Paid

Payments made for customers' property lost or damaged and not covered by insurance should be charged to this account should be credited.

## Professional Fees

All legal fees and expenses other than collection costs, the cost of public accountants' services, the fees of business engineering firms and the cost of similar professional services should be charged here.

## Protective Service

This account should be charged with the cost of any police and security guards, fire or burglar alarms and armored car or special detective service. Fees for bank deposit pickup will also be charged to this account.

## Sales Taxes

Any sales tax paid to a state or municipal government which has not been recovered from the customer should be charged here. If the restaurant chooses to absorb the sales tax in the price of meals or drinks at the bar, this is an administrative decision; this item would then become an administrative expense under the Uniform System.

## Training Costs

An operator will frequently incur training costs in a variety of situations. New employees, especially upon the opening of a restaurant, may be required to participate in a training program. The cost of the training program, including the employees' salary during the program, is charged here.

If a restaurant is staffed for a week or two prior to its opening for training of the cooks and wait staff, the related charges, including salaries, food used in training, related employee meals and the cost of salaries of the trainers should be charged to this account. If preferable, these training costs, as well as similar pre-opening costs, may be capitalized as an asset and amortized over a period of time of 12 months or less. This amortization should be recorded as a direct operating expense.

Employees, particularly management, may attend outside seminars, and the cost of those seminars is included in this account.

## Personnel Expenses

The proper recruiting, training and supervision of employees in restaurants is a task of increasing importance. In larger operations the requirements may warrant setting up a personnel office and a separate account for the expenses involved. The cost of staff-training programs, health examinations, help-wanted advertising, personnel travel, employment agency fees and other expenses of obtaining employees are to be charged to this account.

## Corporate Overhead

Fees charged by a management organization or by the central office of a chain operation for executive supervision and management (commonly called management fees) should be charged to this account. Monthly or other periodic franchise fees are also charged to this account.

Franchisees are generally required to pay a substantial up-front fee for the purchase of the franchise. This fee should be capitalized as an other asset in the balance sheet and amortized over a period of years, generally 10 years or less, to this account.

## Miscellaneous

This category is to take care of the relatively small charges for all items which are administrative or general in nature and are not included under any other captions in this section. For example, such items as the following would be included here:

bank charges
car, bus or taxicab fares
safe-deposit box rentals

Exhibit M
# Repairs and Maintenance

|  | Amounts |
|---|---|
| Painting and Decorating | $ |
| Repairs to: | |
| Dining Room Furniture | |
| Dishwashing and Sanitation Equipment | |
| Kitchen Equipment | |
| Office Equipment | |
| Refrigeration | |
| Air Conditioning | |
| Plumbing and Heating | |
| Electrical Systems | |
| Elevators and Lifts | |
| Floors and Floor Coverings | |
| Buildings | |
| Gardening and Grounds Maintenance | |
| Parking Lot Repairs | |
| Building Alterations Not in the Nature of an Improvement | |
| Plastering | |
| Upholstering | |
| Mending Curtains, Drapes and Hangings | |
| Maintenance Contracts: | |
| Elevators | |
| Signs | |
| Office Machinery | |
| **Total Repairs and Maintenace** | **$_____** |

## Repairs and Maintenance

The items listed in Exhibit M are fully descriptive of the costs and expenses to be charged to this account.

# Occupancy Costs and Depreciation

|  | Amounts |
|---|---|
| OCCUPANCY COSTS: | |
| Rent—Minimum or Fixed Amount | $ |
|   Additional Percentage Rental | |
| Ground Rent | |
| Equipment Rental | |
| Real Estate Taxes | |
| Personal Property Taxes | |
| Other Municipal Taxes | |
| Insurance on Building and Contents | _____ |
| **Total Occupancy Costs** | $_____ |
| | |
| DEPRECIATION: | $ |
| Buildings | |
| Amortization of Leasehold Improvements | |
| Furniture, Fixtures and Equipment | _____ |
| **Total Depreciation** | $_____ |

## Occupancy Costs and Depreciation

### Rent

Leases of land, buildings or equipment are classified as either capital or operating leases. A capital lease meets at least one of the following criteria: a) the leased item becomes the property of the lessee by the end of the lease; b) the lease contains an option to allow the lessee to purchase the leased property at a bargain price defined as substantially less than its fair value at the end of the lease; c) the term of the lease is equal to or greater than 75% of the estimated economic life of the leased property; or d) the present value of the lease payments is equal to or greater than 90% of the fair value of the leased property. A detailed discussion of capital leases and their treatment is outside the scope of this material. For purposes of this discussion, we will assume that all leases are operating leases.

Rent paid to the lessor for the use of the premises is charged here. If it is a percentage lease, it may be desirable to show the minimum rental and the additional percentage rental separately in the schedule. If the rent is for the ground only, the account should be titled ground rent. Rental charges for parking spaces or equipment, such as point-of-sale devices and EDP equipment, should also be charged here. Any payments on local taxes or insurance, which must be made by the tenant under the terms of the lease, should be shown separately and are not to be included in this amount.

### Property Taxes and Property Insurance

Because many of the items included in this group may be paid in a lump sum for a six-month period, a year or, in the case of insurance, a three-to five-year period, the charge to expense should be pro-rated so that each month or year bears its proportionate share of the cost. If these items are charged to expenses in the month in which they are paid, the operating result shown in the statement of income will be distorted.

### Real Estate Taxes

Taxes assessed on the land and buildings by a state, county or city government will be included in this classification if they are to be paid by the lessee or if the property is owned by the restaurant operator.

Special assessments for public improvements are ordinarily considered an increase in the value of the property, and this type of tax should not be included under this heading but charged to the land account.

## Personal Property Taxes

Taxes assessed on personal property and payable by the restaurant operator are charged to this account.

## Other Municipal Taxes

Charges made by a municipality for use of sewers are to be charged here. Some municipalities may have a similar form of property service tax; the amount assessed and payable by the restaurant operator will be charged to local property taxes.

## Insurance on Buildings and Contents

The cost of insurance coverage on the buildings and contents against damage or destruction by fire, water, tornado, sprinkler leakage, boiler explosion or plate glass breakage is properly charged to this account if it is to be paid by the restaurant operator.

## Depreciation—General

The building, furniture and equipment, leasehold and leasehold improvements, which represent a large part of the investment in the business, have an economic life. They will ultimately be disposed of or replaced because they have outlived their usefulness. The costs charged against operations in the statement of income represent the pro-rated recovery of the cost of these items, which is called depreciation.

## Building Depreciation

The estimated decrease in the value of the buildings used by the restaurant operator due to obsolescence should be charged to this account if they are owned by the restaurant.

## Amortization of Leasehold

The costs of acquiring a lease and the expenses incidental thereto, originally charged to an asset account, should be extinguished proportionately over the life of the lease by charges to this expense account.

## Amortization of Leasehold Improvements

The costs of permanent improvements made to leased property, originally charged as assets, are recovered by proportionate charges to this account, either over the remaining life of the lease or over the estimated useful life of the improvement, whichever is shorter.

## Furniture, Fixtures and Equipment Depreciation

The estimated decrease in the value of the furniture, fixtures and equipment resulting from wear and tear and obsolescence will be charged to this account. This account should not include the reduction in value of linen, china, glassware, silver and similar operating equipment, which should be accounted for as suggested in the direct operating expenses section.

# Other Income

| | **Amounts** |
|---|---|
| Service Charges—Net | $ |
| Cover and Minimum Charges | |
| Banquet Room Rentals | |
| Gift and Merchandise Shop | |
| Rental on Shops and Display Cases | |
| Concession Rentals | |
| Vending Machine Commissions | |
| Telephone Commissions | |
| Salvage and Waste Sales | |
| Cash Discounts | |
| Other Miscellaneous Items | _____ |
| **Total Other Income** | $_____ |

## Other Income

All of the restaurant operating income, other than food and beverage sales, are included in this category, as indicated in Exhibit O.

A gift and merchandise shop can be a profitable operation in many cases. Close inventory monitoring and periodic accounting are advisable. Gross profit can be determined through a separate schedule or statement, illustrated as follows:

| **Gift and Merchandise Shop** | **Amounts** | **Ratios to Sales** |
|---|---|---|
| SALES: | | |
| Gift and Novelties | $ | % |
| Sundries | | |
| Candy and Gum | | |
| Tobacco | _____ | _____ |
| **Total Sales** | _____ | _____ |
| | | |
| COST OF SALES: | | |
| Gifts and Novelties | | |
| Sundries | | |
| Candy and Gum | | |
| Tobacco | _____ | _____ |
| **Total Cost of Sales** | _____ | _____ |
| | | |
| **Gross Profit to Other Income** | $_____ | _____ % |

Frequently, a restaurant may sell merchandise such as t-shirts, hats, salad dressings, salsa or a variety of other items. In these instances, it is helpful to specifically identify these items in this schedule.

In some instances the cost of book matches is charged to the gift shop although, in many instances, this item is considered a direct operating expense and classified under supplies. If used outside the restaurant as an advertising medium, book matches should be charged to advertising in the marketing expense category. In large operations, grease sales are sometimes credited to food cost, but in the small restaurant it is practical to include sales of grease along with that of waste paper and bottles in other income. Cash discounts, if they are recorded, may be included in this income group. In most small restaurants, however, it is more practical to consider these discounts as a reduction of the cost of the item purchased and to enter only the net amount paid on the invoice on the cash disbursement sheet.

Exhibit P

# Interest

INTEREST:
Notes                                        $
Long-term Debt
Other                                        _____
   **Total Interest**                        $_____

## Interest

Charges to these accounts include interest expense on bonds, mortgages, notes, equipment contracts, loans and any other debt incurred by the operator in financing the restaurant. It is sometimes helpful to show the amount of interest on each obligation separately.

## Income Taxes

Every organization must pay income taxes on taxable income, and the amount of these taxes is as much a cost of doing business as any other expense item shown on the statement of income. In the case of partnerships, it may not be practical to show these taxes on the restaurant operating statement since the individuals involved may have other items of taxable income or loss that will affect the amount of income tax to be paid. In a corporation's statements, provision for state and federal income taxes are included in the statement of income.

# RATIO ANALYSIS

Ratio analysis allows users of financial information to compare related facts reported in financial statements and review significant relationships between two amounts. Through a review of these relationships, a user can more accurately assess the financial strength of an operation and can compare it to corresponding ratios in prior periods, of other restaurants or industry averages, or of budgeted or planned amounts.

Ratios, however, are only indicators. When a ratio varies significantly from that of a prior period or a budgeted amount, management must investigate the reasons for the difference and take whatever corrective actions may be needed.

## Working Capital

Working capital is the excess of current assets (cash, receivables, marketable investments, inventories and prepaid expenses) over current liabilities (accounts payable, accrued expenses and current portion of loans).

The illustrative balance sheet in Chapter II of this book shows working capital as follows:

| Balance Sheet | Current Assets | Current Liabilities | Working Capital (Deficiency) |
|---|---|---|---|
| Exhibit R | $107,750 | $111,750 | $(4,000) |

In the restaurant operations used as an example in Exhibit R, the existence of a working capital balance indicates an ability to meet all current obligations from the proceeds of current assets. In Exhibit R, however, there are deficiencies of working capital despite that in this example the restaurant is meeting its obligations on time and taking advantage of cash discounts. In fact, in Exhibit R you will note that cash-on-deposit represents 33% of the current assets. While these illustrations are not intended to represent average circumstances, they do indicate that it is possible to operate in the restaurant business with much smaller working capital than is usually the case in mercantile and manufacturing enterprises, where larger sums are required to finance accounts receivable and inventories.

## The Current Ratio

A banker may, upon looking over a balance sheet, talk about the current ratio, which is a term commonly used in discussing one's ability to meet obligations as they come due. The current ratio is arrived at by dividing the current assets by the current liabilities. In normal mercantile or manufacturing businesses, the ratio of 2 to 1, which means that there are two dollars in current assets for every dollar in current liabilities, would be considered a good liquid financial condition. Creditors rely more on the ability of debtors to pay their obligations out of the proceeds of current operations and less upon the debtor's ability to pay in case of liquidation. This may also affect the banker's analysis of financial condition because the restaurant business provides a steady flow of cash from current operations. As stated earlier, many restaurants operate successfully on a current ratio of less than 1 to 1, as a result of collection of receipts (cash or credit card) more quickly than its bills are required to be paid.

The current ratios for the balance sheet used in Chapter II of this book are calculated as follows:

| Balance Sheet | Current Assets | Current Liabilities | Current Assets to Current Liabilities |
|---|---|---|---|
| Exhibit R | $107,750 | $111,750 | .96 to 1 |

These illustrations are not intended to be typical nor do we advocate operating a business on a small cash margin. To do this successfully, there must be relative certainty that business will continue to be good and that the future income will be sufficient to meet today's obligations. Under-capitalization is a fairly common deficiency in restaurants. Insufficient capital causes an operator to curtail marketing progress and service in an attempt to meet fixed obligations. Such curtailment affects the quality of the restaurant, which in turn will further limit income. Capital is essential to support initial progress and pay obligations during periods when sales may be down.

## Inventory Turnover

The rate of inventory turnover, which is an index often used in food and beverages control to determine the efficiency of operation, is determined by dividing the gross cost of food sales by the average inventory.

The following calculations illustrate how the food turnover is calculated:

| Food Operations | Food Costs Including Employees' Meals | Assumed Average Food Inventory | Annual Inventory Turnover |
|---|---|---|---|
| Exhibit Q | $360,500 | $12,250 | 29 Times |
| Exhibit V | 250,160 | 8,900 | 28 Times |

The inventory turnover on beverages is similarly calculated as follows:

| Beverage Operations | Beverage Cost | Assumed Average Beverage Inventory | Annual Inventory Turnover |
|---|---|---|---|
| Exhibit Q | $68,240 | $8,500 | 8 Times |

Because in a beverage operation a relatively larger stock must be maintained than in the food operation, the beverage inventory turnover is usually much smaller than is shown for a food operation.

## Breakeven Analysis

The breakeven point of a restaurant is the dollar amount at which the restaurant's total revenues equal total costs. Breakeven analysis is an important tool to assist the operator in planning for future operations.

Variable costs are those which increase or decrease in proportion with the level of sales. For example, as more meals are sold, the cost of food rises proportionately. Fixed costs are costs which remain constant regardless of the changes in sales activities. For example, insurance expense, property taxes, depreciation expense and interest expense are fixed costs. Some costs may have characteristics of both fixed and variable costs; for purposes of performing a breakeven analysis, the fixed and variable components of these costs must be estimated.

The formula for determining the breakeven point is:

$$\text{Breakeven Point} = \frac{\text{Fixed Costs}}{\text{Contribution Margin Percentage}}$$

The contribution margin percentage is the percent of each revenue dollar which is available to pay fixed costs. The contribution margin percentage may be calculated as follows:

$$\text{Contribution Margin Percentage} = \frac{\text{Total Revenue–Variable Costs}}{\text{Total Revenue}}$$

To illustrate, we will use the statement of income presented earlier in this section as Exhibit B, and will assume (for simplification only) that all costs, except for interest and depreciation, are variable. The contribution margin percentage would then be calculated as follows:

$$\text{Contribution Margin Percentage} = \frac{(\$850,000 + \$2,500)-(\$297,500 + \$517,400-\$16,500-\$4,250)}{(\$850,000 + \$2,500)}$$

$$= \frac{\$58,350}{\$852,500}$$

$$= .0684 \text{ or } 6.84\%$$

Therefore, in our example, after covering variable costs, 6.84% of each sales dollar is available to cover fixed costs.

The breakeven point can now be calculated by dividing fixed costs by the contribution margin percentage calculated above. Using our same assumptions that interest and depreciation are variable costs for purposes of illustration, the breakeven point is calculated as follows:

$$\text{Breakeven Point} = \frac{\$4,250 + \$16,500}{.0684}$$

$$= \frac{\$20,750}{.0684}$$

$$= \$303,362$$

Therefore, in our example this restaurant will break even at $303,362 in total revenue.

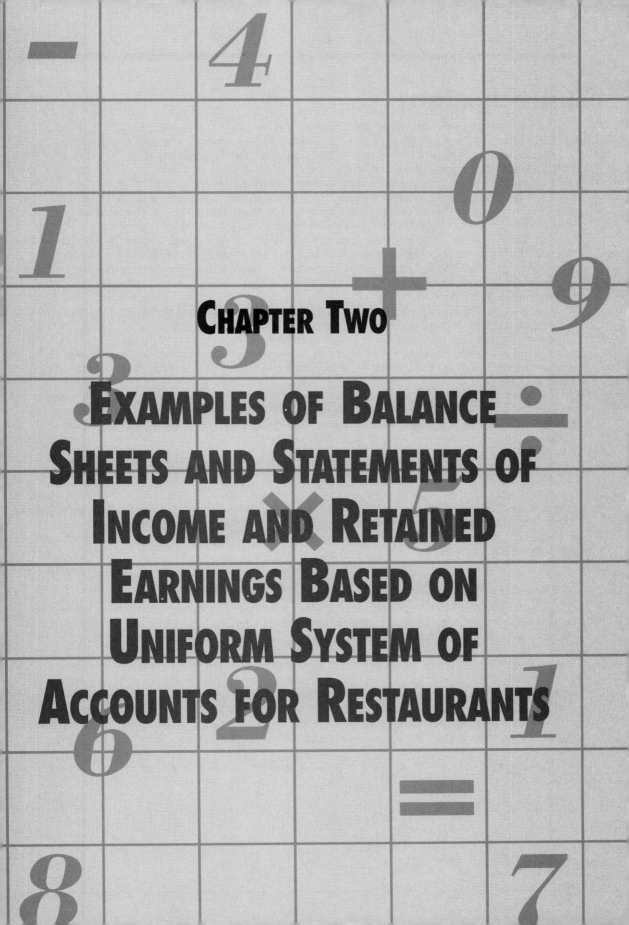

# CHAPTER TWO

# EXAMPLES OF BALANCE SHEETS AND STATEMENTS OF INCOME AND RETAINED EARNINGS BASED ON UNIFORM SYSTEM OF ACCOUNTS FOR RESTAURANTS

# Introduction

To illustrate the practical application of the *Uniform System of Accounts for Restaurants*, this section contains sample statements of several types of restaurants to be used as guides.

The operating results of restaurants depend on the location, type of patronage, physical layout, facilities, local wage rates and labor conditions, rent paid and other factors. Therefore, the exhibits in this section are intended only to show how the form of statement recommended under the *Uniform System of Accounts for Restaurants* can be used. The restaurant types were selected primarily to illustrate the versatility of the system, and the results shown in the exhibits are not intended to be typical or attainable or desirable goals for the restaurant operator.

For a complete analysis of restaurant operations data, we suggest obtaining the most recent copy of the *Restaurant Industry Operations Report*, prepared for the National Restaurant Association, by Deloitte & Touche LLP. Copies of the most current report are available from the National Restaurant Association, 1200 Seventeenth Street, N.W., Washington, DC 20036-3097, telephone (202) 331-5900.

In making comparisons of the trends in the operating results of a restaurant between one period and another or of the figures of one restaurant with another, it will be quite helpful to translate the dollar figures into percentages or ratios to total sales.

A ratio is usually calculated and expressed as a percentage of sales by dividing the dollar amount of each item on the statement of income by the dollar amount of sales and multiplying the result by 100.

By using percentages or ratios to sales rather than dollar amounts, a restaurant operator is in a position to discuss food costs, payroll costs and other operating expenses without disclosing any dollar amounts that might be considered confidential. The Uniform System promotes a set of common terms for the various expenses, and the use of percentages provides a common basis for discussion.

Both the dollar amounts and the ratios or percentages are used in the illustrations that follow.

Ratios may also be used in comparing the operating results of one month or one year of operations with another, since the ratios are easier to keep in mind than the dollars and cents figures. Moreover, ratios indicate more clearly the relationship of the various expenses to the sales of each period, how fluctuations in sales volume affect the costs and the extent to which changes in costs affect the net income.

## Statement of Income for a Full Service Restaurant

Exhibit Q is a statement of income prepared in summary form, showing sales from food and beverages. The base for all ratio computations is total sales, and all of the figures are shown in relation to total sales in the percentage column. For example, the salaries and wages cost of $386,250, divided by the sales figure of $1,287,500, is .30, which multiplied by 100 is 30%. The salaries and wages cost is thus said to be 30 cents per dollar sale, or 30% of sales.

The cost of employees' meals was not calculated, and so the food cost is the gross cost or cost of food consumed. The food and beverage costs are segregated so that the individual cost and gross profit ratios can be determined. Other income includes the gross profit on the gift and sundry shop. Ratios were not calculated for the individual expense items under the direct operating expenses category because the total is relatively small and serves as an adequate measure.

This statement of income does not contain provisions for corporate overhead or income taxes.

Exhibit Q
# Statement of Income
# For Full Service Restaurant
# Serving Food and Beverages

| | Amount | Percentages* |
|---|---|---|
| **SALES:** | | |
| Food | $1,030,000 | 80% |
| Beverage | 257,500 | 20 |
| **Total Sales** | **1,287,500** | **100** |
| **COST OF SALES:** | | |
| Food | 360,500 | 35 |
| Beverage | 68,240 | 27 |
| **Total Cost of Sales** | **428,740** | **33** |
| **GROSS PROFIT:** | | |
| Food | 669,500 | 65 |
| Beverage | 189,260 | 73 |
| **Total Gross Profit** | **858,760** | **67** |
| **OPERATING EXPENSES:** | | |
| Salaries and Wages | 386,250 | 30 |
| Employee Benefits | 51,500 | 4 |
| Direct Operating Expenses | 77,250 | 6 |
| Music and Entertainment | 1,300 | 00.1 |
| Marketing | 25,750 | 2 |
| Utility Services | 38,600 | 3 |
| Repairs and Maintenance | 25,800 | 2 |
| Occupancy | 90,200 | 7 |
| Depreciation | 25,500 | 2 |
| General and Administrative | 39,000 | 3 |
| Other Income | (6,440) | 00.5 |
| **Total Operating Expenses** | **754,710** | **59** |
| **Operating Income** | **104,050** | **10** |
| **Interest** | **6,500** | **00.5** |
| **Income Before Income Taxes** | **$    97,550** | **8%** |

*All ratios are calculated as a percentage of total sales except food and beverage costs, which are based on their respective sales.

## Example Balance Sheets and Detailed Statement of Income Schedules

Exhibit R is the balance sheet of a restaurant operated on a lease basis by a corporation. Because it is a corporation, the statements show a provision for incomes taxes and corporate overhead.

Exhibits S, T and U are detailed schedules of food sales, direct operating expenses and administrative and general expenses, respectively, for a full service restaurant with food and beverage sales.

# Balance Sheet
# Full Service Restaurant with Food and Beverage Sales
# As of (Insert Date)

## Assets

| | | | |
|---|---|---|---|
| CURRENT ASSETS: | | | |
| Cash: | | | |
| House Banks | $ 3,250 | | |
| Cash in Bank | 35,500 | $ 38,750 | |
| Accounts Receivable: | | | |
| Credit Card Receivables | 18,250 | | |
| Customer—House Accounts | 2,500 | 20,750 | |
| Inventories: | | | |
| Food | 15,250 | | |
| Beverage | 8,500 | | |
| Other | 6,000 | 29,750 | |
| Prepaid Expenses | | 18,500 | |
| **Total Current Assets** | | | **$107,750** |
| | | | |
| FIXED ASSETS: | | | |
| Land-Parking Lot | | 58,750 | |
| Leasehold Improvements | | 213,000 | |
| Furniture and Fixtures | | 135,000 | |
| Operating Equipment | | 73,750 | |
| Less: Accumulated Depreciation | | | |
| and Amortization | | (164,750) | 315,750 |
| | | | |
| Other Assets | | | 32,500 |
| | | | |
| **TOTAL ASSETS** | | | **$456,000** |

## Liabilities and Shareholders' Equity

CURRENT LIABILITIES:

| | | |
|---|---:|---:|
| Accounts Payable | $61,000 | |
| Current Portion of Long-Term Debt | 10,500 | |
| Accrued Expenses | 25,500 | |
| Other Current Liabilities | 14,750 | |
| **Total Current Liabilities** | | **$111,750** |
| | | |
| Long-Term Debt, Less Current Portion | | 169,250 |
| Other Noncurrent Liabilities | | 31,250 |
| **Total Liabilities** | | **312,250** |
| | | |
| SHAREHOLDERS' EQUITY | | |
| Capital Stock | 34,000 | |
| Retained Earnings | 109,750 | |
| **Total Shareholders' Equity** | | **143,750** |
| | | |
| **TOTAL LIABILITIES AND SHAREHOLDERS' EQUITY** | | **$456,000** |

Exhibit S
# Food Sales

| | Meals Served | Amounts | Percentages |
|---|---:|---:|---:|
| BY MEAL PERIOD: | | | |
| Lunch | 28,200 | $ 286,230 | 28% |
| Dinner | 57,125 | 733,770 | 71 |
| **Total** | **85,325** | **1,020,000** | **99** |
| | | | |
| Banquets | 500 | 10,000 | 1 |
| **TOTAL MEALS SERVED** | **85,825** | **$1,030,000** | **100%** |

| | Meals Served | Amounts | Percentages |
|---|---:|---:|---:|
| BY LOCATIONS: | | | |
| Dining Room | 65,347 | $ 785,200 | 76% |
| Patio | 20,478 | 244,800 | 24% |
| **TOTAL MEALS SERVED** | **85,825** | **$1,030,000** | **100%** |

Exhibit T
# Direct Operating Expense
## Full Service Restaurant Serving Food and Beverages

| | Amounts | |
| --- | --- | --- |
| | Current Year | Prior Year |
| Uniforms | $ 1,100 | $ 1,200 |
| Laundry and Linen | 9,500 | 9,400 |
| China and Glassware | 9,700 | 9,500 |
| Kitchen Utensils | 3,900 | 3,500 |
| Cleaning Supplies | 3,500 | 3,400 |
| Paper Supplies | 18,500 | 17,500 |
| Bar Expenses | 5,350 | 5,300 |
| Menus and Wine Lists | 3,100 | 3,000 |
| Contract Cleaning | 6,000 | 5,700 |
| Exterminating | 2,000 | 2,000 |
| Flowers and Decorations | 2,500 | 2,600 |
| Auto Expenses | 2,800 | 2,100 |
| Licenses | 2,300 | 2,000 |
| Banquet Expenses | 1,900 | 2,000 |
| Other Operating Expenses | 5,100 | 3,550 |
| **TOTAL DIRECT OPERATING EXPENSE** | **$77,250** | **$72,750** |

Exhibit U
# Administrative and General Expenses
## Full Service Restaurant Serving Food and Beverages

| | Current Year | Prior Year |
| --- | --- | --- |
| Stationery and Office Supplies | $ 2,200 | $ 2,000 |
| Computer Costs | 4,100 | 4,000 |
| Postage | 200 | 400 |
| Telephone | 4,000 | 3,300 |
| Dues and Subscriptions | 800 | 800 |
| Traveling Expenses | 1,700 | 1,500 |
| General Insurance | 6,000 | 5,800 |
| Commissions on Credit Card Charges | 11,000 | 10,400 |
| Doubtful Accounts | 400 | 800 |
| Cash Shortages | 300 | 400 |
| Legal and Accounting Fees | 5,000 | 5,000 |
| Protective Bank Pickup | 1,900 | 1,500 |
| City Sales Taxes | 800 | 800 |
| Other | 600 | 900 |
| **TOTAL ADMINISTRATIVE AND GENERAL EXPENSES** | **$39,000** | **$37,600** |

## Statement of Income for Limited Service—Fast Food Restaurant and Accompanying Schedules

Exhibit V is a summary statement of income for a limited service, fast food restaurant, serving food only. This statement includes a schedule of food costs of various commodity groups typical of fast-food operations. Paper goods are included in the cost of sales because of the direct relationship to food cost.

This illustration also serves to show the adaptability of the form of the statement to the wide variety of restaurants which make up the membership of the National Restaurant Association and, at the same time, the advantages that may accrue to the restaurant when the *Uniform System of Accounts for Restaurants* is used.

Exhibits W, X, Y, Z, AA and BB illustrate detailed schedules for cost of food sales, salaries and wages, direct operating expenses, marketing expenses, utility expenses and general and administrative expenses. These exhibits include only the current month and corresponding percentages.

Exhibit V

# Summary Statement of Income
# Limited Service: Fast Food Restaurant Serving Food Only

|  | Amounts | | Ratios | |
|  | Current Year | Prior Year | Current Year | Prior Year |
|---|---|---|---|---|
| **SALES:** | | | | |
| Food | $641,100 | $600,000 | 100.00% | 100.00% |
| **COST OF SALES:** | | | | |
| Food | 250,160 | 231,000 | 39.02 | 38.50 |
| Paper | 11,680 | 12,000 | 1.82 | 2.00 |
| Total Cost of Sales | 261,840 | 243,000 | 40.84 | 40.50 |
| **Gross Profit** | **379,260** | **357,000** | **59.16** | **59.50** |
| **OPERATING EXPENSES** | | | | |
| Salaries and Wages | 132,340 | 121,200 | 20.64 | 20.20 |
| Employee Benefits | 18,400 | 16,500 | 2.88 | 2.75 |
| Direct Operating Expenses | 11,270 | 10,800 | 1.76 | 1.80 |
| Marketing | 55,930 | 51,600 | 8.72 | 8.60 |
| Utility Services | 17,790 | 15,000 | 2.77 | 2.50 |
| Occupancy Costs | 45,920 | 45,580 | 7.16 | 7.60 |
| Depreciation | 13,680 | 13,300 | 2.13 | 2.22 |
| General and Administrative | 9,970 | 8,800 | 1.55 | 1.46 |
| Repairs and Maintenance | 7,840 | 6,900 | 1.22 | 1.15 |
| Other Income | (800) | (780) | (.12) | (.13) |
| **Total Operating Expenses** | **312,340** | **288,900** | **48.71** | **48.15** |
| Operating Income | 66,920 | 68,100 | 10.44 | 11.35 |
| Interest | 9,620 | 7,200 | 1.50 | 1.20 |
| **Income Before Income Taxes** | **57,300** | **60,900** | **8.95** | **10.15** |
| Income Taxes | 12,830 | 17,650 | 1.99 | 2.94 |
| **NET INCOME** | **$44,470** | **$43,250** | **6.96%** | **7.21%** |

Exhibit W

# Cost of Food Sales
## Limited Service: Fast Food Restaurant
## Serving Food Only

|  | Amounts | Ratios |
|---|---|---|
| Meat and Beef | $108,030 | 16.85% |
| French Fries | 23,990 | 3.74 |
| Produce | 13,780 | 2.15 |
| Produce Salads | 10,700 | 1.67 |
| Salad Bar Ingredients | 11,020 | 1.72 |
| Cheese | 10,190 | 1.59 |
| Chicken | 10,190 | 1.59 |
| Shortening and Oils | 4,810 | .75 |
| Dairy Products | 11,540 | 1.80 |
| Buns | 12,250 | 1.91 |
| Beverages | 10,260 | 1.60 |
| Other Food | 23,400 | 3.65 |
| **TOTAL COST OF FOOD SOLD** | **$250,160** | **39.02%** |

Exhibit X

# Salaries and Wages
## Limited Service: Fast Food Restaurant
## Serving Food Only

|  | Amounts | Ratios |
|---|---|---|
| Service | $ 75,400 | 11.76% |
| Preparation | 9,280 | 1.45 |
| Administrative and general | 33,100 | 5.16 |
| Other | 14,560 | 2.27 |
| **TOTAL SALARIES AND WAGES** | **$132,340** | **20.64%** |

Exhibit Y

# Direct Operating Expenses
## Limited Service: Fast Food Restaurant
## Serving Food Only

|  | Amounts | Ratios |
|---|---|---|
| Uniforms | $2,500 | .39% |
| Kitchen Utensils | 1,800 | .28 |
| Supplies | 3,200 | .50 |
| Contract Cleaning | 800 | .12 |
| Freight | 1,600 | .25 |
| Licenses and Permits | 700 | .11 |
| Miscellaneous | 670 | .11 |
| **TOTAL DIRECT OPERATING EXPENSES:** | **$11,270** | **1.76%** |

## Marketing
## Limited Service: Fast Food Restaurant,
## Serving Food Only

| | Amounts | Ratios |
|---|---|---|
| SELLING AND PROMOTION: | | |
| Direct Mail | $2,820 | .44% |
| Entertaining and Sales Promotion | 5,700 | .89 |
| **Total Selling and Promotion** | **8,520** | **1.33** |
| | | |
| ADVERTISING: | | |
| Newspaper and Magazines | 1,940 | .30 |
| Outdoor Signs | 1,180 | .18 |
| Radio and TV | 3,520 | .56 |
| Programs and Directories | 190 | .03 |
| **Total Advertising** | **6,830** | **1.07** |
| | | |
| FEES AND COMMISSIONS: | | |
| Franchise Fees | 21,700 | 3.38 |
| Agency Fees | 15,360 | 2.41 |
| **Total Fees and Commissions** | **37,060** | **5.79** |
| | | |
| **Other** | **3,520** | **.53** |
| | | |
| **TOTAL MARKETING** | **$55,930** | **8.72%** |

## Utility Services
## Limited Service:
## Fast Food Restaurant,
## Serving Food Only

| | Amounts | Ratios |
|---|---|---|
| Electricity | $12,780 | 1.98% |
| Water | 1,270 | .20 |
| Waste Removal | 1,460 | .23 |
| Gas | 2,090 | .33 |
| Other | 190 | .03 |
| **TOTAL UTILITY SERVICES** | **$17,790** | **2.77%** |

# General and Administrative Expenses
## Limited Service: Fast Food Restaurant, Serving Food Only

|  | Amounts | Ratios |
|---|---|---|
| Insurance–General | $2,500 | .39% |
| Cash Shortages | 1,110 | .17 |
| Professional Fees | 1,020 | .16 |
| Protective Services | 1,800 | .28 |
| Bank Deposit Pickup Services | 1,640 | .26 |
| Telephone | 1,000 | .16 |
| Data Processing Costs | 600 | .09 |
| Miscellaneous | 300 | .04 |
| **TOTAL GENERAL AND ADMINISTRATIVE EXPENSES** | **$9,970** | **1.55%** |

# CHAPTER THREE

# SIMPLIFIED RECORD KEEPING FOR RESTAURANTS

# Introduction

The suggested forms contained in this section are intended to provide the restaurant operator with a complete picture of the business by providing the data needed for the preparation of helpful financial statements. The forms illustrated may in some instances be more detailed than is necessary, in which case the restaurant operator will use those columns and spaces to fit individual needs. The information put on these forms comes from data generated by basic routines and equipment, including point-of-sale terminals (cash registers), checkbook or voucher systems, payroll records, and the paid and unpaid invoice files.

Report preparation is a step which requires a person with some technical and bookkeeping talents; however, no attempt is made in this text to explain any technical accounting points, such as the difference between the cash basis or accrual basis of accounting, the use of prepaid or accrued expenses, allowance for depreciation, or the like. In the event the owner or manager is not familiar with bookkeeping methods, we suggest that a part-time bookkeeper be employed to make the necessary closing entries each month. The operator has another choice for preparation of the financial statements since the statement can be prepared by using a software package. All current and comparative data required can be prepared using software, assuming accurate basic data is provided by someone at the restaurant.

A statement of income is a summary in dollars and cents of the operating transactions of a restaurant made during the period of time it covers. To reflect the financial results of operations in the restaurant business, as in any other, certain adjustments must be made to the accumulated daily figures compiled during the month by the owner or bookkeeper. These adjustments are recorded in a general journal, Form 6, explained in this section. Since most adjustments are of a routine nature, most can be made by a bookkeeper with proper and regular review. However, unless statements are prepared purely on a cash receipts and disbursements basis, someone with a knowledge of double-entry bookkeeping will be required to prepare or to explain what is to be done. It is also obvious that this book cannot be a bookkeeping text. The primary purpose for this section is to illustrate how a good record of daily transactions will aid the operators of smaller restaurants. They will then be in a position to have proper statements prepared with a minimum of work on the part of a bookkeeper or accountant at the end of the month or at the end of the fiscal year.

Most businesses are conducted to produce income; consequently, the owner is vitally interested in how much money is made or lost. A prudent restaurant operator is also interested in how the restaurant's results compare with a predetermined profit plan. These are questions readily answered by analyzing the operating results reflected in the statements based on data made available from a simple but adequate record-keeping system, summarized and adjusted by a bookkeeper. The extent of available information on sales, food costs, other expenses and profits depends on the amount of detail made available by the records.

The object of the forms outlined in this section is primarily to place the restaurant operator in a position, with only a few entries each day, to have the records necessary to accumulate the daily transactions that will facilitate preparation of a monthly statement. Thus, all of the instructions in connection with these forms are directed toward the daily use of the sample forms by the owner, manager or someone delegated for the task. If the entries are made daily, correct record keeping will not be a burden or nuisance, and the owner can easily keep abreast of the business as it progresses. This section also attempts to free the restaurant owner of the thought that bookkeeping and bookkeepers are a necessary nuisance continually annoying them with detail. Our purpose is, instead, to implant the idea that properly compiled figures can become an invaluable tool in improving a business situation. That is why the earlier statement was made that the bookkeeping forms, as outlined, were designed to give complete detail on operations, if desired. Also, the forms are flexible enough so that the user can eliminate any detail and retain only that part which is practical in each particular case.

# Recommended Forms for Use in Simplified Record Keeping for Restaurants

The forms recommended for implementation of this simplified record-keeping system are summarized below and fully discussed in the text that follows.

The six major forms can be written up on accounting columnar paper and bound into one ledger. Each should have an appropriate identification tab. These are the permanent records required. The sources of the data used on each major form are preliminary forms or records, such as the cash register, cash count and deposit recapitulation, bank checkbook or voucher register, payroll summary records and invoice files. Each of these is used to support the permanent records.

| Number | Major Form | Source Record |
|--------|-----------|---------------|
| Form 1 | Sales and Cash Receipts | Daily Report (Form 1-B) |
| Form 1-A | Cashier's Summary | Cash Register Report Tapes |
| Form 1-B | Daily Report | Cashier's Summary (Form 1-A) |
| Form 2 | Cash Disbursements | Checkbook or Check Vouchers |
| Form 3 | Record of Unpaid Bills (Accounts Payable) | Unpaid Invoice File |
| Form 4 | Salaries and Wages Worksheet and Check Register | Time Cards or Time Book; Employee Payroll Records |
| Form 5 | Employment Record | Employee Payroll Records; Salaries and Wages Worksheet and Check Register |
| Form 6 | General Journal | Inventories; Accrual Information |

The source records have value in addition to supporting figures for the permanent records. For example, Form 1-A, Cashier's Summary, provides a record of currency, bank checks, credit cards by company and the total bank deposit. This form provides for the shifts of four cashiers, each with independent over or short verification.

The Daily Report, Form 1-B, is an important document because current and cumulative data vital to the restaurant operation are recorded here. The daily report generally includes food and beverage sales by meal period. The illustrated report also indicates sales by type of beverage and shows how to back out sales tax if it is included in the sales price of beverages. The back page of the daily report shows accounts receivable charges, collections and a recapitulation control account. Details of other income and allowances are also included. It is recommended that a record of sales by meals and the customer count be kept as an additional tool for management to facilitate the analysis of the fluctuations in expenses and changes in restaurant profit. The daily report form also provides a record of cash paidouts. If this form is not used, some type of memorandum book should be kept in which to record this information.

Data in the cash summary and paid-out sections of the daily report are recorded in the Sales and Cash Receipts Journal, Form 1, providing a permanent record for compiling the monthly totals. The operator of a small restaurant serving food only and interested in daily cash sales will not need to use the daily report form but can make the daily entries directly into the Sales and Cash Receipts Journal, Form 1, using cash register summary tapes.

At the close of the month, the proprietor or part-time bookkeeper will need to prepare journal entries to be recorded in the general journal. Also, a general ledger will be required for posting the transactions affecting asset and liability accounts. A part-time bookkeeper will then have the required figures to prepare the financial statements. If, however, the statement is to be prepared by an outside data processor, only a general journal is required. A sample of this journal is shown in Form 6. The general ledger will be a computer-prepared printout, a copy of which will be returned to the restaurant at the end of each accounting period. If the daily work is kept up-to-date, a bookkeeper need spend only a few hours at the end of the month; it should be fairly easy to find someone to do this work on a part-time basis. For convenience, the columns in each form are numbered so that they can be more easily understood by a person not trained in bookkeeping methods and to facilitate use of the data for computer input.

# Sales and Cash Receipts--Form 1

## (Source Records Are Forms l-A and 1-B)

Sales and cash receipts are recorded on Form 1. The form is used to segregate sales into various categories, such as food, beverage, gift and miscellaneous sales, and also to record sales taxes, payments on customers' accounts, and items that must be paid for with cash. In very small restaurants, the permanent record of cash receipts might be a simple cash book in which each day's receipts are recorded or, if the operator wishes to separate cash sales from cash received from other sources, two account columns and a descriptive column. However, most restaurants, large or small, use cash registers to record daily sales, sales taxes, charges, tips, paidouts and more. A summary of each of the transactions of each cashier is then required. Form 1-A is an illustration of a cashier's summary report.

Cash registers and electronic point-of-sale terminals produce summary printouts and verification against which actual cash and charges turned in by the cashiers are measured. Where these machines are used, the illustrated cashier's summary may not be required.

## Form 1-A—Cashier's Summary

This form is divided into two parts. Part I is simply a summary of currency, silver, checks and charges which make up the deposit. Part II is the cash summary or verification that sales plus sales tax are accounted for by the receipt of either cash or credit card vouchers. Opening and closing register readings should also be recorded to make certain no transactions took place between periods of operating the registers. Some cashier's summaries also show these data; others use the daily report, Form 1-B. Form 1-A is also divided into five columns, four representing each of four cashier shift periods and a fifth summarizing all four shifts.

The cashier assigned to each day shift turns in currency, silver, credit card vouchers and bank checks in a deposit envelope after counting out the fund used to make change. A responsible person other than the cashier reads the cash register and removes the tapes (optional) at the close of each shift. The receipts, charge vouchers and checks are deposited in a secure place, preferably a safe. This routine is followed for each cashier on each shift. The following day, the person responsible (a clerk, manager, bookkeeper or head cashier) removes the cashier's envelope, counts the cash, summarizes the credit card vouchers, lists the bank checks and records the amounts on Part I of Form 1-A, lines 2 through 12.

The next procedure is to remove the tapes from the cash register (unless done at the close of the shift). The sales and sales taxes are recorded on Part II, lines 14 and 15. They are adjusted on lines 17-20 for over or short rings, transfers or other differences. The result will be the sales and sales tax to be accounted for on lines 21 and 22. Other additions are made, if applicable, on lines 23 through 32 and then totaled on line 33. Paidouts, tips paid out and house charges (lines 34, 35 and 36) are totaled (line 37) and deducted from total receipts (line 33). The result is the net cash receipts (line 38). The bank deposit (line 12, Part I) is compared with net cash receipts (line 38), and the difference is recorded on line 40 (over) or short. These differences generally require explanations by the cashier.

The summary column may be used to record receipts not rung up on the register (lines 23, 24 and 25). This procedure is sometimes preferred to not commingle other receipts with daily register transactions. Data from the summary column E is transferred to the cash summary section on the daily report.

The use of Form 1-A pinpoints responsibility, provides control and summarizes information for use in preparing the daily report.

## Cashier's Summary

DATE _____  DAY _____  PREPARED BY _____

| | (A) | (B) | (C) | (D) | (E) |
|---|---|---|---|---|---|
| | Bar Register | | Service Register | | Total |
| | Day | Night | Day | Night | All Shifts |
| 1. **Bank Deposit** Part I | | | | | |
| 2. Currency | | | | | |
| 3. Silver | | | | | |
| 4. Checks | | | | | |
| 5. Subtotal | | | | | |
| 6. Credit Cards: | | | | | |
| 7. MasterCard/Visa | | | | | |
| 8. American Express | | | | | |
| 9. Diners Club | | | | | |
| 10. Other | | | | | |
| 11. Other Receipts: | | | | | |
| 12. Total Bank Deposit | | | | | |
| | | | | | |
| 13. **Cash Summary** Part II | | | | | |
| 14. Sales per Register | | | | | |
| 15. Sales Tax per Register | | | | | |
| 16. Adjustments: | | | | | |
| 17. Over/Under Rings | | | | | |
| 18. Other: Complimentaries | | | | | |
| 19. Other | | | | | |
| 20. Total Adjustments | | | | | |
| 21. Sales to be Acctd. for | | | | | |
| 22. Sales Tax to be Acctd. for | | | | | |
| 23. Accounts Collected | | | | | |
| 24. Other Receipts: | | | | | |
| 25. | | | | | |
| 26. | | | | | |
| 27. Tips Charged: | | | | | |
| 28. MasterCard/Visa | | | | | |
| 29. American Express | | | | | |
| 30. Diners Club | | | | | |
| 31. Other | | | | | |
| 32. House Accounts-Tips | | | | | |
| 33. Total Receipts | | | | | |
| 34. Deduct: Paidouts | | | | | |
| 35. Tips Paid Out | | | | | |
| 36. House Charges | | | | | |
| 37. Total Deductions | | | | | |
| 38. Net Cash Receipts | | | | | |
| 39. Bank Deposit (Line 12) | | | | | |
| 40. (Over) or Short | | | | | |

In operations where only one cash register or one shift is needed, the cashier's summary record with only one column will be adequate. Many cash registers and most point-of-sale terminals are programmed to produce a summary report of transactions. This process may require the insertion of a preprinted report form, or the report may be printed on the register tape. Transaction reports, if available as described, provide all the data and more than cashier's reports did prior to the electronic age. In fact, several types of reports can be produced in addition to the cashier's summary, including productivity by hour or shift or the grand total.

The following information is available from one type of point-of-sale terminal. It illustrates the detail and control that can be provided. Owners will want to contact various manufacturers and review their equipment before making a purchase.

### Cashier's Report

(From an electronic, point-of-sale terminal)
    Report number—Cashier
        Mode (Read or Reset)
        Void Counter
        Void Total
    No Sales Count
        Daily Sales/Gross Total
    Service Charges Collected
    Total Cash Collected
    Total Checks Collected
    Total American Express Collected
    Total MasterCard/Visa Collected
    Previous Balance/Balance Forward
    Total Discounts
    Sequence Number
        Register Number
        Date

## Form 1-B Daily Report

The daily report is used for management information purposes and as a source document for recording sales and cash receipts data. This report is completed at the time the deposit is made, using data from the cashier's summary report and from cash register tapes. Then at a later and more convenient time, the information can be transcribed on Form 1, the sales and cash receipts. The figures used in the daily report can be written on plain columnar paper or memorandum sheets or can be amplified as illustrated in Form 1-B. The illustrated report includes sales by meal periods divided among food, beverage, gifts and miscellaneous, sales taxes, accounts receivable collections, the number of persons served, other receipts, paidouts and bank deposit information.

The detail required to make sound management decisions should be the criteria for how much data should be included in the daily report. Point-of-sale-terminals provide a wealth of information not readily available from mechanical registers. Operators of the smallest of restaurants can have adequate daily reporting without sophisticated bookkeeping systems if full use is made of these machines.

# Daily Report

Day _____ Weather _____ Events _____ Date _____

| Sales and Sales Tax Collected | Bar Register | | Service Register | | Totals | | Last Month To Date |
| --- | --- | --- | --- | --- | --- | --- | --- |
| By Source | Lunch | Dinner | Lunch | Dinner | Today | Month To Date | |
| 1. | | | | | | | |
| 2. Food Sales: | | | | | | | |
| 3. Regular Menu | | | | | | | |
| 4. Oyster Bar, Other | | | | | | | |
| 5. Total Food Sales | | | | | | | |
| 6. Beverage Sales: | | | | | | | |
| 7. Liquor | | | | | | | |
| 8. Beer | | | | | | | |
| 9. Wine | | | | | | | |
| 10. Soda, Other | | | | | | | |
| 11. Total Including Sales Tax | | | | | | | |
| 12. Sales Tax on Beverage Sales | | | | | | | |
| 13. Total Beverage Sales | | | | | | | |
| 14. Total Food & Beverage Sales | | | | | | | |
| 15. Gift Shop & Misc. Sales | | | | | | | |
| 16. Total Restaurant Sales | | | | | | | |
| 17. Sales Tax Collected | | | | | | | |
| 18. Adjusted Sales and Sales Tax per Cashier's Summary | | | | | | | |

NOTE: When printing this form for restaurant use, this page and the one following should be both placed on one page with the back page on the reverse side.

# Daily Report

| 19. | Cash Summary | Amount |
|---|---|---|
| 20. | Food Sales | |
| 21. | Beverage Sales | |
| 22. | Gift Shop & Misc. Sales | |
| 23. | Sales Tax: | |
| 24. | Food | |
| 25. | Beverage | |
| 26. | Gift Shop & Misc. Sales | |
| 27. | Accounts Collected (Over) | |
| 28. | Other Receipts (Over) | |
| 29. | Tips Charged | |
| 30. | Total Receipts | |
| 31. | *Deduct:* | |
| 32. | Paid Outs (see Detail) | |
| 33. | Tips Paid Out | |
| 34. | House Charges | |
| 35. | Allowance/Complimentaries | |
| 36. | Total Deductions | |
| 37. | Net for Deposit | |
| 38. | Bank Deposit | |
| 39. | (Over) or Short | |

| | | Customers Served | | | Average Check | |
|---|---|---|---|---|---|---|
| | | Today | This Month To Date | Last Month To Date | This Month | Last Month |
| 40. | Meal Period: | | | | | |
| 41. | Lunch | | | | | |
| 42. | Dinner | | | | | |
| 43. | Total | | | | | |

## Sales Summary

| 44. | | | | | |
|---|---|---|---|---|---|
| 45. | Meal Period | Today | This Month To Date | This Year To Date | Last Year To Date |
| 46. | Food: | | | | |
| 47. | Lunch | | | | |
| 48. | Dinner | | | | |
| 49. | Oyster Bar, Other | | | | |
| 50. | Total | | | | |
| 51. | Beverage: | | | | |
| 52. | Lunch | | | | |
| 53. | Dinner | | | | |
| 54. | Total | | | | |
| 55. | Gift Shop & Misc. | | | | |
| 56. | Grand Total | | | | |

| | Paidouts | Food | Other | Total |
|---|---|---|---|---|
| 57. | | | | |
| 58. | | | | |
| 59. | | | | |
| 60. | | | | |
| 61. | Total Paidouts | | | |

**Daily Report**
(continued)

**Back Page**

Day _____                                    Date _____ , 19____

| Check Number | Customers' Accounts Charged | Total Amount Charged | | Tips Charged | |
|---|---|---|---|---|---|
| | | | | | |
| | | | | | |
| | | | | | |
| | | | | | |
| | | | | | |
| | Total Accounts Charged | | | | |

| Other Receipts | Amount | |
|---|---|---|
| | | |
| | | |
| | | |
| | | |
| | | |
| | | |
| | | |

| Customers' Accounts Collected | Amount | |
|---|---|---|
| | | |
| | | |
| | | |
| | | |
| | | |
| | | |
| | | |

| Allowances/Complimentaries | | | |
|---|---|---|---|
| Name | Reason | Amount | |
| | | | |
| | | | |
| | | | |
| | | | |
| | | | |
| | | | |
| | Total | | |

| Accounts Receivable | Amounts | |
|---|---|---|
| Balance Yesterday | | |
| Today's Charges | | |
| Total | | |
| Today's Collection | | |
| Allowances | | |
| | | |
| Balance Today | | |

_____

_____

Prepared by: _____        Date Prepared: _____

The daily report, Form 1-B, was designed to cover the needs of the owner of a medium-sized restaurant who requires details about sales and customers and whose operations include food, beverage, gift shop and miscellaneous sales. The policy is to extend credit to an occasional customer, and sales are controlled by cash registers and guest checks.

## Sales and Sales Tax Collected by Source

The restaurant for which this daily report was designed has two cash registers, one located at a stand-up public bar and one at a service bar. In addition, a precheck register is located in the kitchen.

Numbers are taken off cash and precheck register tapes, which are "Z'd" or closed out at the end of each cashier's shift. Most registers can be preprogrammed or preset to individual pricing specifications and still allow good flexibility in operation. The descriptions here, including the daily report, are only samples for demonstration purposes. Most register manufacturers will demonstrate a variety of equipment with wide variations in sophistication.

Food sales, line 2, are taken off a tape from the precheck register. Beverage sales are taken from a similar tape from both service and bar registers. Sales tax is added to the checks of customers served at tables; however, beverage sales at the bar include the sales tax, making it necessary, in this instance, to "back-out" the sales tax (see line 12). Beverage sales by group must also be adjusted by the applicable sales tax.

The figures on these tapes have been previously adjusted to compensate for over or under rings and other adjustments. This process was undertaken at the time of the daily cashiers' audit and was reflected on the cashier's summary report, Form 1-A, lines 17, 18 and 19. Thus the total of all sales and sales tax collected on line 18 of the daily report, Form 1-B, should equal lines 20, 21 and 22 on the cashier's summary report, Form 1A.

Food sales on the daily report, Form 1-B, are listed according to the type of menu and by meal period from each cash register (lines 2, 3 and 4). Beverage sales are broken down by category (lines 6, 7, 8, 9 and 10) for both lunch and dinner for both bar and service registers. When the service bar is not open for lunch, all beverage sales are recorded through the bar register. Gift shop and miscellaneous sales are recorded on line 15, using special keys on the service register. Applicable sales tax is added.

Total restaurant sales, line 16, is the result of adding lines 5, 13 and 15. These data are summarized for today, month to date and last month to date.

In restaurants with cash registers that are not preset, the cashier will enter the price, add the check at settlement, add the sales tax and then total. The total will be rung on the register as either cash or charge. This is still standard procedure in many restaurants and requires a cashier's report, showing all charge checks, and also requires auditing checks to be sure pricing is correct. Human error in pricing, totaling and summarizing makes this process less flexible and more time-consuming than a preset pricing system.

## Cash Summary

This section of the daily report, Form 1-B, is identical to the cashier's summary report, Form 1-A, except that the cash summary includes data from all four cashier shifts. The results for each shift are summarized on lines 20 through 39. The total receipts (line 30) are reduced by paidouts and other deductions, resulting in the net cash receipts for the entire restaurant on line 37. The bank deposit (line 38) is compared with the net cash receipts. Any difference will be an overage or shortage in the cash and is shown on line 39.

## Customers Served

A section on the front page of the daily report is made available to accumulate the number of customers served and to record the average check. Lunch and dinner statistics are illustrated; however, other meal periods may be added as required. The average for any one day is not significant due to variations in customers' selections. The average check to date is an important indicator of menu popularity and menu pricing and reflects the effect of price changes and promotions. The number of customers served may reflect the strength or weakness of economic and other trends, providing there were no severe policy changes.

## Sales Summary

The sales by meal period of food, beverage, gifts and miscellaneous for each day are shown in this section. The month to date is compared with the current fiscal year and the prior year. Total restaurant sales, less allowance for inflation, are the true barometer of growth and public acceptance or lack of growth and customers' apathy. Every operator strives to improve sales each year to provide growth for the organization and to cover the inevitable increase in expenses. This section contains the data for measuring results.

## Paidouts

The record of transactions in which cash is paid out is at the bottom of Form 1-B. The name of the payee, a description of the item paid for and the amount paid are recorded. It is advisable to use a petty cash voucher as a memorandum for such payments. These forms are standard at most stationers and provide for the date, name, description of item paid for and the amount paid, as well as a space for the name of the person receiving the money and for approval of the disbursement.

## Form 1-B (BACK PAGE)

A record of customer accounts charged and collections plus detail of other income, is kept on the reverse side of the daily report. These schedules are described below.

## Customers' Accounts Charged

Space is provided to list the customers' checks charged, showing check number, name, total charge (including tip) and tip only. The amount due from credit card agencies is also recorded if the restaurant is on a delayed payment plan.

Complimentary charges are not written up in this section but under allowances. Complimentary charges will be written off at the end of the accounting period.

## Accounts Collected

Provision is made for entering the information on customer accounts collected, including receipts from credit card companies. When payment is received from a credit card company, the check will usually be net of the collection fee charged. The gross amount of customers' accounts is usually shown as a memorandum on the stub or voucher check, less the fee. The gross amount should be recorded as collected accounts, and the fee should be recorded as an allowance to be later charged to credit card commissions in the administrative and general section of the income statement.

## Other Receipts

Other receipts consist of vending machine commissions, telephone commissions, grease sales, discount checks and similar receipts not directly related to sales. These receipts may originate with one or more of the cashiers or may be received by mail and added to the report by the preparer. The source and amount of such receipts are recorded in this space.

## Accounts Receivable

A section has been provided in which to summarize the charge account transactions for the day. To yesterday's balance of uncollected accounts, today's charges are added. Today's collections or allowances are deducted to arrive at the total of uncollected receivables at the end of the day. Allowances or adjustments of accounts receivable are sometimes necessary as a matter of policy or to reflect the cost of commissions to credit card agencies. It may also sometimes be necessary to write an account off as uncollectible. These allowances must be journalized by the bookkeeper at the end of the month to keep the accounts receivable from customers in balance. The practical entry for allowances in a small operation would be to charge these write-offs and adjustments to administrative and general expense and to credit customers' accounts receivable.

Gathering daily information on sales and cash receipts is greatly facilitated through the use of both the cashier's summary and the daily report. The cashier's summary serves as a control over the transactions and cash while the daily report provides needed operating data, as well as income data for the permanent records.

## Preparation of Sales and Cash Receipt- Form 1

This form is the permanent record of sales and cash received. A sample is included in this text. It is possible and practical, of course, to use any columnar book or set of rule sheets, such as are obtained in any local stationery store, by heading up the columns as suggested or as they may be changed to suit individual needs.

The purpose of this sales and cash receipts form is to accumulate the daily sales and cash receipts in their proper categories so that the totals of the columns will show the monthly receipts, charges and collections on customers' accounts and cash deposited. The source of the amounts is the daily report, Form 1-B, or the source could be simply a cash register-produced form or tape. Each of the columns in Form 1 will be described in the following text because for most restaurants this form represents a minimum requirement. However, in a very small operation the proprietor may not want to go to the trouble of dividing the sales between food, beverage and other. In that case, it is quite probable that the cash receipts will represent the sales for the day. Also, in that case, there may be occasional items representing cash received, such as advances of additional capital investment, repayment of loans made to employees or others, or sales of old equipment, and these items should be shown separately under other receipts. Therefore, some restaurant operators may require only the following columns: food sales, miscellaneous sales, sales tax, other tax, other receipts, total receipts, cash paid out, cash over or short, and bank deposit.

If a cash register is used, it is possible to separate the sales for breakfast, lunch and dinner by reading the register at the end of each meal period. Guest checks can be used in making this division by separating them into appropriate categories. Cash registers or point-of-sale terminals provide for divisions between food, beverage, gift or miscellaneous sales, sales tax, and tips charged. Guest checks also facilitate the compilation of a count of the number of customers served, although many registers are also designed to provide the number of customers in addition to cash totals. Thus, both register and guest checks can be used to amplify the daily accumulation of information on sales, as well as to serve their primary function, which is the internal control of sales. Form 1 can be contracted or expanded to suit the needs of each restaurant. In the following paragraphs, the various columns in Form 1 are discussed.

## Column 1—Date

As a rule only one line on the form will be required for each day but more may be used if necessary. For instance, it may be necessary to use two or more lines to describe miscellaneous receipts.

## Column 2—Food Sales

Enter the total food sales for the day in this column.

## Column 3—Beverage Sales

If liquor, beer or wine is sold, it is highly advisable to separate these sales from the food sales. The manner of separation is not covered here since it is assumed that if the volume of these sales is enough to separate, it will be possible to do so by cash register, guest checks or otherwise. In any event, beverage sales will include soft drinks but not coffee, tea or milk, which are included in food sales.

Separate columns will be necessary for each category of beverage sales if this is desirable. This may be accomplished by lengthening the sales portion of this form or by keeping a subsidiary record that ties in with column 3. The daily report, Form 1-B, is an illustration of a subsidiary record that shows the types of beverage sold.

## Column 4—Gift Shop and Miscellaneous

Many restaurants have a counter at the cashier's stand for the sale of gifts, tobacco and candy. These sales are recorded separately from food and beverage sales, and a separate column is provided on this form to record them.

## Columns 5 and 6—Sales Tax Collected

In many states and municipalities, sales tax is collected from the customer and is accounted for separately. For this reason, a separate column is provided for the sales tax relating to different categories of sales. Also, some states have different tax rates for different sales; therefore, two or more columns for sales tax should be provided. In this case, column 5 is for tax collected on food and miscellaneous; column 6 is for tax collected on beverages.

Tax collections kept separately will be credited to a sales tax account in the general ledger, and amounts paid to the government will be charged to this same clearing account.

Sales tax should not be charged against administrative and general or any other expense classification. If sales tax is included in the sales prices, then the tax portion should be calculated and sales reduced by that amount. The inclusion of sales tax in the sales will affect the food cost and expense ratios because sales will be inflated.

## Column 7—Accounts Collected

The daily total of collections from customers' charges made on prior days is recorded in this column. These collections are not a part of today's sales, and for that reason the cash received must be shown separately in order to keep the correct sales totals.

Collected accounts, in this instance, refer only to house charges collected and do not refer to credit card collections unless the restaurant is on a weekly or longer payment basis with one of the credit card agencies. The restaurants that have an agreement for immediate payment with these agencies treat credit card charges like cash and deposit the charges daily; therefore, there are no future collections of this type of charge.

House charges and extended credit card arrangements are grouped as accounts charged, column 15. It is the payment of this type of charge that is recorded in column 7 when collected. An example of this type of record is included on the back page of the daily report, Form 1-B. The record should include the customer's name and amount of the collection.

## Column 8—Tips Charged

The policy of allowing the customer to obtain meals on credit by signing the check also poses the problem of what to do when the amount of a tip is added to the check, which has become the prevailing procedure. Usually these tips are paid out of the cash drawer to the server, who signs a tip voucher as a receipt. This also makes it necessary in the daily records to provide separate columns in which to record the amount of tips charged and the tips paid columns 8 and 14, Form 1, are provided for this purpose.

The daily total of all tips added to charge checks by customers will be recorded in column 8. The total of this column will be credited to a clearing account in the general books, offset by the total of the tips paid, column 14.

Since the cashier will ordinarily keep all charge checks and credit card vouchers separate from the cash sales, the total amount of tips charged can be transcribed from the checks as the charges are listed. The cashier's summary sheets generally provide the data for compiling these records. Tip recording is illustrated on the cashier's summary, Form 1-A.

## Columns 9 and 10—Other Receipts

Enter in these columns the sales of items other than food, beverage, gift or miscellaneous. Such other miscellaneous income items as commissions from vending machines, waste paper and bottle sales, subrentals and cash commissions are entered here. Also enter in these columns any cash receipts that are not ordinarily rung up on the cash register, such as additional investments of the proprietor, loans or sales of equipment. Column 9 is provided for a description of each amount in column 10. More than one line can be used for each if necessary.

## Column 11—Total Receipts

The first ten columns are added, and the total is placed in column 11, which shows the sales and cash receipts to be accounted for on that day. The total receipts should be identical to the amount on line 33 of the cashier's summary, Form 1-A. The first eleven columns are all credits.

The total of columns 13, 14, 15, 16, 17 and 18 also equal the amount shown in column 11; in this manner the transactions are kept in balance. This is the principle of "double-entry book-keeping." The operator is then assured that the receipts have been accounted for correctly.

## Columns 12 and 13—Paidouts

Column 13 is for supplies and services paid out of the cashier's funds. The paidout is explained in column 12.

It is likely, except in the very small restaurant, that the number of petty cash transactions will require more than one line. Therefore, it would be advisable and practical to keep a small memorandum book at the cashier's stand to record and add individual payments. Each day's total may be entered from this memorandum book in columns 12 and 13. At the bottom of these columns after the total for the month is recorded, a summary of the transactions should be made for posting to the general books.

## Column 14—Tips Paid Out

Column 14 is for the tips paid out on credit card guest checks. The total should offset the amount shown in column 8.

## Column 15—Accounts Charged

The total of all charge sales to customers for the day will be recorded in this column. These charges are a part of the day's sales, so the amount must be deducted from the sales to arrive at the net cash receipts. Charge sales from credit card agencies that are deposited daily are not considered charges in this instance. Charges included here are from the credit plan of the restaurant or from other credit card plans where payment is extended beyond one day. The record of such charges is made on the back page of the daily report, Form 1-B. The charge record should at least include the date, the amount charged and the customer's name. In a small restaurant it may not be necessary to send out bills for the few charges made; but if it is necessary to do so, there should be a record of the customer's address and credit card number, if any.

## Column 16—Allowances/Complimentaries

Complimentary charges are recorded under allowances. This occurs because restaurant operators find it advisable at times to "compliment" customers by canceling their restaurant checks. This practice may be for promotional purposes or to adjust an unfavorable situation which developed because of poor service, poor food or both. If complimentary charges have been rung through the cash register, these must be accounted for. These items are treated as allowances and are written off at the end of an accounting period.

## Column 17—(Over) or Short

Errors can be made by servers or by cashiers through over or under rings which were not caught when the cashier's summary report was prepared. It may also be that the cash turned in by the cashier was over or short of the amount to be accounted for. The amount of this difference will be shown in column 17. If the deposit is greater than the sales figure, the difference is considered an overage and is shown in parenthesis. Sometimes the over or short column is placed on the credit side of Form 1 just before total receipts. When this procedure is used, a shortage of sales is shown in parentheses.

## Column 18—Bank Deposit

The bank deposit for each day should be the same amount as shown on the daily report, Form 1-B, line 38. This should be logical since the source data for the sales and cash receipts form is the daily report. The amount in column 18 is the result of reducing total receipts, column 11, by the paidouts, column 13; tips paid out, column 14; accounts charged, column 15; allowance, column 16; plus or minus over or short, intact column 17.

It is advisable that each day's receipts be deposited intact and that all major disbursements be made by check. In the event several days' receipts are deposited at one time, it is advisable to make separate deposit slips, one for each day, so the bank deposits can easily be traced to the sales and cash receipts record, Form 1.

## Sales and Cash Receipts

MONTH _____ , 19___

| (1) Date | (2) Food Sales | (3) Beverage Sales | (4) Gift Shop Miscel- laneous Sales | (5) Sales Tax Collected — Food & Miscel- laneous | (6) Sales Tax Collected — Beverage | (7) Accounts Collected | (8) Tips Charged | (9) Other Receipts — Detail | (10) Other Receipts — Amount | (11) Total Receipts |
|---|---|---|---|---|---|---|---|---|---|---|
| 1. | | | | | | | | | | |
| 2. | | | | | | | | | | |
| 3. | | | | | | | | | | |
| 4. | | | | | | | | | | |
| 5. | | | | | | | | | | |
| 6. | | | | | | | | | | |
| 7. | | | | | | | | | | |
| 8. | | | | | | | | | | |
| 9. | | | | | | | | | | |
| 10. | | | | | | | | | | |
| 11. | | | | | | | | | | |

CREDITS

# Sales and Cash Receipts (cont'd)

DEBITS

| | (12) Paid | | (14) Tips Paid Out | (15) Accounts Charged | (16) Allowances/ Complimentaries | (17) (Over) or Short | (18) Bank Deposit |
|---|---|---|---|---|---|---|---|
| | Detail | (13) Amount | | | | | |
| 1. | | | | | | | |
| 2. | | | | | | | |
| 3. | | | | | | | |
| 4. | | | | | | | |
| 5. | | | | | | | |
| 6. | | | | | | | |
| 7. | | | | | | | |
| 8. | | | | | | | |
| 9. | | | | | | | |
| 10. | | | | | | | |
| 11. | | | | | | | |

# Cash Disbursements—Form 2

The record of cash disbursements shown on Form 2 is a check register and purchase journal, combined for simplicity and the convenience of the restaurant operator. The primary purpose of the form is to provide for the recording of all checks drawn and the classification of the expenditures for statement purposes.

This form has been designed to provide for distribution of expenses with sufficient individual expense columns to keep summarizing to a minimum. The expense columns are grouped according to the Uniform System format, described in Chapters I and II of this text.

Summarizing expenses by assigned account number also facilitates use of this form for computer input. In a small restaurant where only a few invoices are recorded, it may be practical to simply affix the expense code number on the check stub for direct input to the computer. However, in large restaurants this might be impractical. Therefore, some type of summary record, like Form 2, is required.

Although we believe the form illustrated in this text to be a convenient one for the small restaurant operator, a columnar book or set of sheets may be used by merely heading up the various columns as suggested or as they may be changed to suit individual needs.

The checks should be entered in numerical order as each is drawn, and each should be on a separate line. It is advisable to enter each check on the day it is made out. This keeps the record up to date so that at the end of the month it need only be totaled in preparation for computer input or posting to the general ledger.

The first three columns, which are not numbered, are for the date of the check, the name of the payee and the check number, all of which are self-explanatory. The figure columns have been numbered for convenient reference. Each column also is headed by an expense account code number. Where double columns are used, one is for recording the correct expense account code number, and the other is for the amount. Any systematic account numbering system may be used. The one used here is an acceptable standard grouping as further detailed in the appendix.

## Column 1—Amount of Check

Enter here the exact amount of each check drawn.

## Column 2—Accounts Payable

Just as provision was made in the sales and cash receipts, Form 1, for charge sales to be recorded as sales on the day the sale is made even though collected at a later date, some provision must also be made for expenses and other liabilities incurred during the current operating period but which are paid by the restaurant at a later date. Such expenses result in an account payable and should be recorded in the month or period to which they apply. For this reason the record of unpaid bills, Form 3, has been included in this section and will be described later in this text.

If Form 3 is used or if by some similar method a bill or liability has already been recorded on the books in a prior period, the payment of this item will be entered in column 2, accounts payable. If it should happen that a bill which applies to a prior period has not already been entered as an accounts payable, it will, of course, not be entered in column 2 but will be treated as a cost or expense for the current month.

## Column 3—Food Purchases

Enter in column 3 all payments for food purchases which have not already been entered on Form 3 in prior periods. Also enter here the charge for delivery of foodstuffs, freight express and cartage.

## Column 4—Beverage Purchases

If the restaurant includes a bar or cocktail lounge, a separate account should be kept of the beverage purchases. Therefore, column 4 provides for the entry of all payments for beverage purchases which have not already been entered on Form 3 in prior periods.

## Column 5—Gifts and Miscellaneous

If the restaurant sells a sufficient amount of gifts and miscellaneous items, it may be convenient to use this column for recording these purchases. In a small restaurant, if the purchases of tobacco, candy and gifts are infrequent enough, it would be practical to enter them in column 21 under administrative and general, placing a proper account number opposite each entry.

## Column 6—Discounts

In many cases, a purveyor may allow a discount for bills paid within 10 days or within a month. These discounts represent earnings to the restaurant operator and should be included with other income on the operating statement. For this reason column 6 has been provided to record the savings due to prompt payment. This is a credit column.

Many operators do not enter the discounts, feeling that the amounts are too small to warrant accounting for them. In that case, the total and the distribution columns also show the net amount of the check issued in payment of their bills.

## Column 7—Payroll Expense

Enter in this column the amount of all salaries and wages paid. This amount should represent the actual expenses of salaries and wages and will include not only the net wages shown in column 1 but also any taxes withheld shown in columns 8, 9, 10 and 11.

If a payroll record book is used, it may be practical to enter only the total of the payroll as shown in this record. This treatment holds true if a check is drawn to reimburse the payroll bank account, providing one is maintained.

A weekly payroll summary, Form 4, is illustrated later in this text. Form 4 is designed to provide a means of keeping payroll tax and other payroll elements properly entered. This form will facilitate proper recording and will also denote compliance with the federal and state wage and hour regulations.

If the payroll is prepared by a data-processing service, the use of a payroll bank account is also a convenient method of handling this expense. A payroll summary record similar in content to Form 4 is one of the reports provided from an EDP service. In this case, only the net amount of payroll expense is entered in the cash disbursements, column 1, offset by an entry in column 27, general ledger.

If part of a payroll applies to a prior or succeeding month, a journal entry is made (see Form 5) at the end of the month, applying the proper amount to each period for statement purposes. If salaries and wages expense, as well as other expenses, is not accrued, a distortion of the operating results will occur. The subject is mentioned here only to indicate to those familiar with bookkeeping methods that such accruals may be necessary for complete accuracy in recording the payroll expense of each period. The small operator who does not wish to accrue expenses and whose weekly payroll has two or three days run into the following month should not total the cash disbursements record until that payroll has been entered.

## Column 8—Withholding Taxes

Taxes withheld on each employee are listed on the payroll summary record similar to Form 4, illustrated later in this section. The amount of taxes withheld is recorded in column 8 as a credit.

## Column 9 and 10—Payroll Taxes Collected

The amounts entered in these columns also originate from the payroll summary. This represents taxes collected from employees and due to the government. The wage and hour law specifies that tip earnings reported are subject to FICA taxes and are shown separately to facilitate record keeping and show compliance with the law.

Some employers also arrange for their employees to purchase saving certificates on a payroll plan, and others have pension or group insurance plans to which the employees contribute. These deductions can also be shown in additional columns as required. Use of two columns is suggested, one to list the expense account number and one the amount.

# Column 11—Employee Benefits

Payroll taxes and fringe benefits are an important part of the expense of operating any business. Since these costs have a direct relation to the payroll, they are, in effect, a part of the labor cost. To account for these expenses properly, it is advisable to show them separately in the operating statement right next to the cash payroll so that the operator can have a better picture of total labor costs.

Enter in this column the payment of the restaurant's portion of federal retirement tax, federal unemployment tax, state unemployment tax, workmen's compensation insurance and any other fringe benefits the employees may receive as outlined under the heading Employee Benefits in the *Uniform System of Accounts for Restaurants*—Chapter I of this text.

# Columns 12 through 25—Operating Expenses

Enter in these columns all amounts paid for items included under this heading in the *Uniform System of Accounts for Restaurants* in Chapter I of this text. These include:

Columns 12 and 13   Direct Operating Expenses
Columns 14 and 15   Music and Entertainment
Columns 16 and 17   Marketing
Columns 18 and 19   Utility Services
Columns 20 and 21   Administrative and General
Columns 22 and 23   Repairs and Maintenance
Columns 24 and 25   Rent and Other Occupancy Costs

The first column number in the above sequence is used for the appropriate account number or an explanation so that the exact nature of the item entered can be shown. These, in turn, may be summarized at the bottom of the column after it is totaled to provide a more detailed analysis of these expenses.

# Columns 26 and 27—General Ledger

These columns are used for items that do not directly affect the income and expenses of the operations but do affect either assets or liabilities. The principal portion of a note payable, purchase of furniture or equipment, employee advances, prepaid insurance premiums and similar amounts are included here. An explanation of balance sheet items is included in Chapter I of this text.

# General

By the use of the forms shown in this section, the restaurant operator can have a statement prepared showing sales and other income, food and beverage costs, salaries and wages and employee benefits, other controllable expenses, and rent and other occupancy costs. A knowledge of these items is essential to good operations.

The forms are prepared so that the information they provide can be expanded to the extent found convenient in each instance to meet the desire for more detail. These forms have also been prepared to facilitate the use of the figures either for input for a computer-prepared statement or for use by a bookkeeper who would prepare a statement by hand. Many restaurant companies now have on-premise computer systems with restaurant software which incorporates formats to substitute for the forms contained herein.

Form 2

# CASH DISBURSEMENTS

| Date | PAYEE | Check Number | (1) 1100 (CR) Check Amount | (2) 2120 (DB) Accounts Payable | (3) 5100 (DB) Food Purchases | (4) 5200 (DB) Beverage Purchases | (5) 6210 (DB) Gifts and Miscellaneous | (6) 6400 (CR) Discounts | (7) 7100 (DB) Payroll Expense | (8) 2200 (CR) Withholding Taxes | (9) 2220 (CR) FICA Regular | (10) 2260 (CR) FICA Tips | (11) 7200 (CR) Employee Benefits |
|------|-------|--------------|------|------|------|------|------|------|------|------|------|------|------|
| 1. | | | | | | | | | | | | | |
| 2. | | | | | | | | | | | | | |
| 3. | | | | | | | | | | | | | |
| 4. | | | | | | | | | | | | | |
| 5. | | | | | | | | | | | | | |
| 6. | | | | | | | | | | | | | |
| 7. | | | | | | | | | | | | | |
| 8. | | | | | | | | | | | | | |
| 9. | | | | | | | | | | | | | |
| 10. | | | | | | | | | | | | | |
| 11. | | | | | | | | | | | | | |
| 12. | | | | | | | | | | | | | |
| 13. | | | | | | | | | | | | | |

# CASH DISBURSEMENTS (cont'd)

| | Direct Operating | | Music & Entertainment | | Marketing | | Utility Services | | Administrative & General | | Repairs & Maintenance | | Rent & Occupancy Costs | | General Ledger | |
|---|---|---|---|---|---|---|---|---|---|---|---|---|---|---|---|---|
| | (12) 7400 | (13) (DR) 7498 | (14) 7500 | (15) (DR) 7560 | (16) 7600 | (17) (DR) 7643 | (18) 7700 | (19) (DR) 7795 | (20) 7800 | (21) (DR) 7870 | (22) 7900 | (23) (DR) 7998 | (24) 8100 | (25) (DR) 8160 | (26) 1100 | (27) (DR) 9020 |
| | Account Number | Amount | Account Number | Amount | Account Number | Amount | Account Number | Amount | Account Number | Amount | Account Number | Amount | Account Number | Amount | Account Number | Amount |
| 1. | | | | | | | | | | | | | | | | |
| 2. | | | | | | | | | | | | | | | | |
| 3. | | | | | | | | | | | | | | | | |
| 4. | | | | | | | | | | | | | | | | |
| 5. | | | | | | | | | | | | | | | | |
| 6. | | | | | | | | | | | | | | | | |
| 7. | | | | | | | | | | | | | | | | |
| 8. | | | | | | | | | | | | | | | | |
| 9. | | | | | | | | | | | | | | | | |
| 10. | | | | | | | | | | | | | | | | |
| 11. | | | | | | | | | | | | | | | | |
| 12. | | | | | | | | | | | | | | | | |
| 13. | | | | | | | | | | | | | | | | |

# Record of Unpaid Bills—Form 3

At the end of the month or accounting period, there are always some bills for goods or services that were received during the month but not paid and, therefore, not entered in the cash disbursements book. For this reason, Form 3, the record of unpaid bills, has been developed as a means of entering them in the accounts. Unpaid bills are also called accounts payable.

The columns in Form 3 are similar to those in the cash disbursements book, Form 2, and it is not necessary to repeat their explanations here. This form provides for the distribution of these unpaid items to the proper expense categories. Columns 3 to 22 less column 6 should equal column 1. Because of the similarity of Forms 2 and 3, it is also possible to use a separate sheet of Form 2 for recording unpaid bills by a proper use of the columns.

It is assumed that accrued or prepaid payroll will be accounted for by the preparer or bookkeeper as previously explained in connection with the payroll columns, Form 2. This form makes no special provision for unpaid payroll. If it is desirable to enter unpaid payroll here, the distribution can be explained in a column added for that purpose.

The only column that needs an explanation here is the one entitled date paid. Operators in many small restaurants attempt to stay on a cash basis. Thus, when a payment of one of the bills entered on this form is made in the following month or period, it is well to refer to the sheet on which that unpaid bill is listed and to insert in the date-paid column the date on which this bill is paid. This will provide for a continuous day-to-day record of unpaid bills, which will be the ones remaining without any date-paid notation opposite them.

In cases where bills are allowed to remain unpaid for more than a month or partial payments are made, it is advisable to have the record keeper or bookkeeper set up an accounts payable ledger. Ordinarily, in a small operation this should not be necessary, and the open items on Form 3 can be totaled to show the accounts payable.

# Salaries and Wages Records— Forms 4 and 5

Record keeping for salaries and wages is an important function for the restaurant operator because of the need for management information on this significant expenditure and because of the requirements of the Fair Labor Standards Act. The act was amended to include restaurants under the jurisdiction of the U.S. Department of Labor as of February 1, 1967 and as amended again in 1974, 1977 and 1989. The provisions of the act make it mandatory for pay records to reveal data which proves the establishment is in compliance.

Fortunately, the advent of low-cost computers and the development of sophisticated companies which process payrolls and produce all the records required has simplified the task of record keeping somewhat. It is recommended that most restaurants use a service of this type.

We have prepared a sample worksheet and check register, Form 4, and an individual employment record, Form 5, for the guidance of the restaurant operator who finds it advantageous to prepare the records and checks internally. These two forms are designed for use in the average restaurant and may be expanded or reduced as required. Forms 4 and 5 contain column headings which are similar to most computer-prepared forms.

Since most restaurants, particularly the smaller ones, are on a weekly pay basis, the salaries and wages worksheet, Form 4, has been designed accordingly. Where salaries and wages are

# Record of Unpaid Bills

| Date | Name of Creditor | (1) 2120 Accounts Payable | (2) Date Paid | (3) 5100 Food Purchases | (4) 5200 Beverage Purchases | (5) 6210 Gifts and Miscellaneous | (6) 6400 Discounts | (7) 7400 Account Number | (8) 7498 Amount |
|---|---|---|---|---|---|---|---|---|---|
| | | | | | | | | Direct Operating Expenses | |
| 1. | | | | | | | | | |
| 2. | | | | | | | | | |
| 3. | | | | | | | | | |
| 4. | | | | | | | | | |
| 5. | | | | | | | | | |
| 6. | | | | | | | | | |
| 7. | | | | | | | | | |
| 8. | | | | | | | | | |
| 9. | | | | | | | | | |
| 10. | | | | | | | | | |
| 11. | | | | | | | | | |
| 12. | | | | | | | | | |
| 13. | | | | | | | | | |

## Record of Unpaid Bills (cont'd)

| | (9) 7500 | (10) 7560 | (11) 7600 | (12) 7643 | (13) 7700 | (14) 7795 | (15) 7800 | (16) 7870 | (17) 7900 | (18) 7998 | (19) 8100 | (20) 8160 | (21) 1100 | (22) 9020 |
|---|---|---|---|---|---|---|---|---|---|---|---|---|---|---|
| | Music & Entertainment | | Marketing | | Utility Services | | Administrative & General | | Repairs & Maintenance | | Occupancy Costs | | General Ledger | |
| | Account Number | Amount | Account Number | Amount | Account Number | Amount | Account Number | Amount | Account Number | Amount | Account Number | Amount | Account Number | Amount |
| 1. | | | | | | | | | | | | | | |
| 2. | | | | | | | | | | | | | | |
| 3. | | | | | | | | | | | | | | |
| 4. | | | | | | | | | | | | | | |
| 5. | | | | | | | | | | | | | | |
| 6. | | | | | | | | | | | | | | |
| 7. | | | | | | | | | | | | | | |
| 8. | | | | | | | | | | | | | | |
| 9. | | | | | | | | | | | | | | |
| 10. | | | | | | | | | | | | | | |
| 11. | | | | | | | | | | | | | | |
| 12. | | | | | | | | | | | | | | |
| 13. | | | | | | | | | | | | | | |

paid semi-monthly or monthly, the columns outlined can easily be adapted to that policy.

There are many systems, stock forms and employment cards available at printing and stationery houses which may better fit the needs in some cases. The main purpose of the forms outlined here is to indicate how the essential elements making up the cost of salaries and wages can be compiled to indicate compliance with the applicable laws.

There are systems available using compatible forms where the worksheet, employee check and employment record can be made out simultaneously with one entry. This is commonly known as a one-write system and can be used by very small restaurants.

# Salaries and Wages Worksheet and Check Register—Form 4

A separate bank account should be used for payment of salaries and wages. The totals in the respective columns will be tied into the amounts shown in the cash disbursements, Form 2, where the reimbursement check is recorded.

The checks should be entered in numerical order as they are drawn and each given a separate line on the worksheet. It is also suggested that employees be grouped by position using a classification similar to that illustrated in Exhibit 1 of Chapter II in this book or as illustrated in Chapter IV. Division of employees by position makes it easier to analyze the hours worked by comparison to a budget or standard. Each employee group has a definite relationship to sales, number of meals served and productivity, which can more easily be recorded and monitored when employees are grouped by position on Form 4.

The pay period covered will be indicated at the top of the form. The columns for the employee number, name, position and department were not numbered as they do not enter into the computation.

## Columns 1 and 2—Hourly Rate

The wage rate for the regular hours worked or for the period worked (if semi-monthly or other) is entered in column 1. Column 2 is reserved for the overtime wage rate.

## Columns 3 and 4—Hours Worked

The number of regular hours is entered in column 3, and the number of overtime hours is entered in column 4. The record of time will be taken from a time card or a time book kept by the department head, supervisor or other management personnel.

## Column 5—Total Salaries and Wage Expense

Hours worked multiplied by the hourly wage rate is the amount of cash expense to the employer. This total is entered in column 5.

## Column 6—Service Charges

The amount of tips or service charges that are collected by the employer on banquet and other checks and distributed to the employee is shown in column 6.

## Column 7—Total Paid by Employer

The salaries and wages expense, plus the tips and service charges collected and distributed by the employer shown in column 6, is the gross amount due to the employee for his services. The net amount of the check is calculated by taking the employee deductions from this gross figure.

## Columns 8 and 9—Employee Meals and Reported Tips

Columns 8 and 9 are memorandums only and contain information needed to indicate compliance with the minimum wage law and the amounts to be used in computing withholding for federal income taxes and FICA taxes.

The value of employees' meals used for tax purposes is arbitrary and is probably not necessary to meet the minimum wage. The hourly rates for most restaurant employees established by the supply and demand of qualified persons is, in many states, equal to or greater than the minimum wage. Unless it is necessary to provide compliance, the employees' meals valuation, column 9, will not be used.

For federal income tax purposes, tipped employees are required to report to the employer the amount of tips they have received directly from the customers. The amounts are considered in determining withholding taxes. This becomes doubly important in connection with the percentage of tip allowance used in computing compliance with the Fair Labor Standards Act. With a weekly pay period, it is practical to have the employee report weekly.

## Column 10—Wage and Hour Total

The total paid by the employer plus the credits for employee meals and reported tips is the amount indicating compliance with the Wage and Hour Law.

It is also the amount used in computing FICA taxes and federal withholding taxes, subject to the provision of the Internal Revenue Service in regard to meals furnished employees for the benefit of the employer. On such meals the employee is not required, at present, to pay federal income tax.

## Deductions

In Form 4, columns 11 and 12 are provided for the withholding of the employee taxes on income. A third column is provided with a space for a code number for any other payroll deductions such as group insurance, union dues and cash advances. In cases where there are deductions of a weekly recurring nature that would affect the employees' take-home pay, it may be more practical to provide additional columns to cover them. Each type of other deduction is indicated by a code number, and the total is recapped at the bottom of the payroll worksheet.

## Column 11—FICA

The employees' portion of the Federal Insurance Contribution Act (Social Security) is computed and entered in this column.

## Column 12—Withholding Tax

The amount withheld by the employer for the employees' federal income taxes is computed on the basis of the tables, using the number of exemptions as required.

## Columns 13 and 14—Other: Code, Amount

Columns for the code number, amount of other deductions from employees' wages and the total deductions in determining the employees' take-home pay are provided to make it easier to compute net pay.

## Column 15—Total Deductions

## Column 16—Net Pay

The gross amount shown in column 7 less the total deductions shown in column 15 results in the net pay, which is the amount of the check to be issued to the employee.

## Column 17—Check Number

The check number is shown in the last column for practical purposes, such as the bank reconciliation, auditing and proper record keeping.

## General

The total salaries and wages for the period, the total amount of each deduction and the total net pay are amounts posted to the cash disbursements, Form 2, supporting the reimbursement check to the salaries and wages bank account and the entry of the expense into the general accounts.

# Employment Record Form—5

The employment record, Form 5, is designed to become a permanent record of the employee's annual earnings, and it will be one of the major records required in cases involving disputes regarding minimum wages and other employer-employee relationships. As such, this employment record should contain as much information as it is practical to insert on the face of the form, such as:

1.  Employee's full name
2.  Social security number
3.  Most recent address
4.  Telephone number
5.  Department or type of work
6.  Date of birth
7.  Employee number, if used
8.  Number of exemptions for withholding tax purposes
9.  Date of employment
10. Hourly rate of pay and space for any rate changes with the date and space for approval
11. Last date of employment
12. Reason for leaving
13. Nearest relative and address, name and address of person to notify in case of an emergency

Other information that will supplement the employment record, such as the employee's job application form, withholding certificate, record of employee's tips and time cards should be maintained for each employee. While we do not illustrate these various forms in the *Uniform System of Accounts for Restaurants*, they are readily obtainable from stationery stores and the U.S. Government Printing Office.

The example form has been designed to be used with a one-write system along with the payroll worksheet, Form 4, to accumulate quarterly and end-of-calendar-year earnings for the reporting of individual wages to federal and state agencies. Subtotals will be taken at the end of each quarter, thus indicating quarterly totals on the payroll worksheet, Form 4, and the individual earning record, Form 5. Using this procedure, the employer is able to maintain a cumulative total for the purposes of determining the tax liability for federal and state unemployment taxes and the Federal Insurance Contributions Act. With many POS systems available today, this form and related process will be automated.

Payroll records must be kept in such a manner that all provisions of the wage and hour law are fulfilled. If this is done, any subsequent inspection of the employee records by governmental agencies will be facilitated, and complete compliance with the various regulations can easily be determined.

# Salaries and Wages Worksheet and Check Register    Period from _____ to _____

Form 4

| Check No. or ID No. | Name of Employee | Position | Dept No. | (1) Wage Rate Regular | (2) Wage Rate O.T. | (3) Hours Worked Regular | (4) Hours Worked O.T. | (5) Salaries And Wages | (6) Tips & Service Charges | (7) Total Paid by Employer |
|---|---|---|---|---|---|---|---|---|---|---|
| 1. | | | | | | | | | | |
| 2. | | | | | | | | | | |
| 3. | | | | | | | | | | |
| 4. | | | | | | | | | | |
| 5. | | | | | | | | | | |
| 6. | | | | | | | | | | |
| 7. | | | | | | | | | | |
| 8. | | | | | | | | | | |
| 9. | | | | | | | | | | |
| 10. | | | | | | | | | | |
| 11. | | | | | | | | | | |
| 12. | | | | | | | | | | |
| 13. | | | | | | | | | | |

# Salaries and Wages Worksheet and Check Register (cont'd)    Period from _____ to _____

| | (8) | (9) | (10) | (11) | (12) | (13) | (14) | (15) | (16) | (17) |
|---|---|---|---|---|---|---|---|---|---|---|
| | Memo Only | | Wage and Hour Total | FICA | Withholding Tax | DEDUCTIONS | | Total Deductions | Net Pay | Check Number |
| | Employee Meals | Reported Tips | | | | Code | Amount | | | |
| 1. | | | | | | | | | | |
| 2. | | | | | | | | | | |
| 3. | | | | | | | | | | |
| 4. | | | | | | | | | | |
| 5. | | | | | | | | | | |
| 6. | | | | | | | | | | |
| 7. | | | | | | | | | | |
| 8. | | | | | | | | | | |
| 9. | | | | | | | | | | |
| 10. | | | | | | | | | | |
| 11. | | | | | | | | | | |
| 12. | | | | | | | | | | |
| 13. | | | | | | | | | | |

# Employment Record

Name: _____
Address: _____
Date of Birth: _____

Social Security No.: _____
Identification No.: _____
Date of Employment: _____
Last Date of Employment: _____

Position: _____
Telephone: _____
Reason for Leaving: _____

Income Tax Exemptions: _____
Emergency Contact: _____
Name: _____
Telephone: _____

| | Period Worked | | Dept. No. | Wage | | Hours Worked | | Total Salaries and Wages | Distr. Tips and Service Charges | Memo Only | | Wage and Hour Total | Withholding | | | Other | | Total Deductions | Net Pay |
| | Begin | End | | Regular | O.T. | Regular | O.T. | | | Employees Meals | Reported Tips | | FICA | Tax | Code | Amount | | | |
|---|---|---|---|---|---|---|---|---|---|---|---|---|---|---|---|---|---|---|---|
| 1 | | | | | | | | | | | | | | | | | | | |
| 2 | | | | | | | | | | | | | | | | | | | |
| 3 | | | | | | | | | | | | | | | | | | | |
| 4 | | | | | | | | | | | | | | | | | | | |
| 5 | | | | | | | | | | | | | | | | | | | |
| 6 | | | | | | | | | | | | | | | | | | | |
| 7 | | | | | | | | | | | | | | | | | | | |
| 8 | | | | | | | | | | | | | | | | | | | |
| 9 | | | | | | | | | | | | | | | | | | | |
| 10 | | | | | | | | | | | | | | | | | | | |
| 11 | | | | | | | | | | | | | | | | | | | |
| 12 | | | | | | | | | | | | | | | | | | | |
| 13 | | | | | | | | | | | | | | | | | | | |

# General Journal Form—6

At the close of each accounting period, certain adjustments must be made. These adjustments will include the changes in the value of food, beverage and other inventories between the beginning and end of the accounting period. This is true, assuming that regular inventories are taken for control purposes and that the fluctuations are sufficient to affect the food cost and other cost where the amount of goods on hand is a factor. The adjustments will also include a charge to operations to cover the depreciation on the furniture, equipment and the building if they are part of the investment in the business. The amortization of the leasehold and value of improvements made must also be adjusted.

Some of the other expenses, such as insurance, taxes and licenses, are paid on an annual basis. It is usually desirable to apportion them over the period of the monthly statements by an adjustment which would result in charging one-twelfth of the operating cost to the current month. These and other similar items are adjustments which require some experience with double-entry bookkeeping and are necessary for monitoring by a part-time bookkeeper or accountant.

Adjustments are made by means of journal entries. Each account requiring an adjustment has a number assigned to it based on the chart of accounts. Adjustments will either be credits or debits to the ledger account selected.

One type of general journal is illustrated in Form 6. Two columns are used for each set of entries: one credit and one debit. Two sets of columns are used for each month or accounting period. Several accounting periods could be maintained on each page eliminating the need to write the entries each period.

A routine procedure to make the entries can be set up by a bookkeeper and maintained by an administrative assistant or management person; however, a person with bookkeeping knowledge should review the entries for accuracy periodically.

Eleven typical adjusting entries are illustrated on Form 6 and are briefly explained in the following text.

## Journal Entries 1 and 2—Food and Beverage Inventory Adjustment

The inventory figure shown on the balance sheet is the value of the physical count taken at the end of the month or accounting period. The inventory taken at the end of the next period will be either more or less than the beginning inventory. If the ending inventory is more than the beginning one, then the difference will be added to the inventory account, and the cost will be reduced. If the reverse is the case, then the entry is reversed.

## Journal Entry 3—Depreciation

The monthly charge for depreciation is determined on the basis of the estimated useful life. This journal entry is used to record the expense for each period and to increase the allowance account, which shows the portion of the total investment that has been recovered.

## Journal Entries 4 and 5—Accrued Salaries and Wages

Most restaurant operators pay their employees weekly. Since interim accounting periods are usually monthly, the number of days paid may not correspond to the days of operation. It is important to match all expenses against sales for like periods; otherwise, the statement of income may be widely distorted. It is necessary, therefore, to make a journal entry. The following procedures may be used.

A.   There will usually be a journal entry in the general journal from the previous month. It will be a credit to accrued salaries and wages and a debit to the respective expense accounts. The first step is to reverse this entry. This is done by simply reversing the debits and the credits.

B.   The second step is to set up the accrual for the current month by (a) crediting the accrued payroll account and debiting the payroll expense accounts. The easiest way to calculate the amount to be used is to divide the last payroll for the final week of the period by seven (or the number of operating days per week). Do this for each employee category. This will give the expense for one day. Multiply the daily expense for each category by the number of days to be accrued. Record the results in the journal entry.

## Journal Entry 6—Cost Transfers

Cost ratios for food and beverage are sensitive measurements of operations. Transfers of food to bar or from beverages to food will affect the cost. Therefore, when these transfers are substantial, it is advisable to allocate the cost to the appropriate department. The journal entry illustrated accomplishes this.

## Journal Entry 7—Allowances and Complimentaries

Complimentary food and beverage amounts should be accumulated during the accounting period and then expensed. The ratio between the complimentary food sales and beverage sales should be tested periodically to determine the appropriate percentage to be allocated to food costs and beverage costs.

## Journal Entry 8—Accrued Percentage Rent

Restaurant leases may have a base rent versus a percentage-of-sales rent. The percentage rent may be due monthly, quarterly or annually. It is necessary to expense the percentage rent payable during the accounting period in which the sales were recorded.

## Journal Entry 9—Commission on Credit Card Charges

Credit card companies charge a fee or discount rate for credit card handling. The fee is usually a percentage of credit card sales. The credit card sales are transferred to the restaurant's bank account net of the fee. This entry expenses the credit card commissions and any bank's service charges for the accounting period.

## Journal Entry 10—Real Estate Taxes

Property taxes are typically paid two times a year. A portion of the property tax is accrued for each accounting period. If the property taxes are paid in advance, the prepaid taxes account is offset, and if the taxes are deferred, the accrued taxes account is utilized.

## Journal Entry 11—Sales Tax on Beverage Sales

When the price of a beverage includes sales tax, the sales tax liability must be extrapolated from the beverage sales. For example, a beverage sells for $4.00 and the sales tax rate is 6%. The $4.00 is divided by 1.06 to determine that the sales tax liability is $.23. ($4.00÷1.06 = $3.77; $4.00–$3.77 = $.23)

## General

There are several more journal entries that may be made, depending on the circumstances. The company's public accountant will be helpful in making these determinations.

## General Journal

| Entry No. | | Account Code Number | Month Dr. | Cr. |
|---|---|---|---|---|
| #1 | Cost of Food | | XX | |
| | Cost of Beverage | | XX | |
| |   Inventory--Food | | | XX |
| |   Inventory--Beverage | | | XX |
| | To Reverse Last Month's Entry | | | |
| #2 | Inventory--Food | | XX | |
| | Inventory--Beverage | | XX | |
| |   Cost of Food | | | XX |
| |   Cost of Beverage | | | XX |
| | To Reflect Current Inventory | | | |
| #3 | Depreciation | | XX | |
| |   Accumulated Depreciation | | | XX |
| | To Record Portion of Cost of Building and Equipment Recovered During Month | | | |
| #4 | Accrued Salaries and Wages | | XX | |
| |   Administrative | | | XX |
| |   Preparation | | | XX |
| |   Bar | | | XX |
| |   Service | | | XX |
| | To Reverse Entry for Prior Month (If Any) | | | |
| #5 | Administrative | | XX | |
| | Preparation | | XX | |
| | Bar | | XX | |
| | Service | | XX | |
| |   Accrued Salaries and Wages | | | XX |
| | To Record Expense for Period to be Paid Next Period | | | |
| #6 | Cost of Beverage | | XX | |
| |   Cost of Food | | | XX |
| | To Record Net Value of Transfers Between Departments | | | |
| #7(a) | Food Sales | | XX | |
| | Beverage Sales | | XX | |
| |   Allowances and Complimentaries | | | XX |
| | To Remove Complimentaries and Allowances From Sales | | | |
| #7(b) | Complimentary Food and Beverage | | XX | |
| |   Cost of Food | | | XX |
| |   Cost of Beverage | | | XX |
| | To Transfer the Cost of Food and Beverage Associated with Complimentaries to a Marketing Sub-Account | | | |

## General Journal

| #8 | Percentage Rent | | XX | |
|---|---|---|---|---|
| | Accrued Rent | | | XX |
| | To Record Percentage Rent (If Any) | | | |
| #9 | Commissions on Credit Card Charges | | XX | |
| | Bank Charges | | XX | |
| | Cash on Deposit | | | XX |
| | To Record Credit Card and | | | |
| | Bank Charges per the | | | |
| | Bank Statement Reconciliation | | | |
| #10 | Real Estate Taxes | | XX | |
| | Prepaid (or Accrued) Taxes | | | XX |
| | To Record Monthly Expenses | | | |
| | for Real Estate Taxes | | | |
| # 11 | Beverage Sales | | XX | |
| | Sales Tax Payable | | | XX |
| | To Record Sales Tax Liability | | | |
| | When the Price of the Beverage | | | |
| | Includes Sales Tax | | | |

# Point of Sale Systems

Technology is used today in restaurants to improve sales and service while decreasing labor cost and increasing efficiency. Key management areas in which restaurants are investing their technology dollars are point of sales, purchasing and ordering, labor scheduling, menu planning and inventory tracking. With rapidly decreasing prices for improving technology, the small operator has the opportunity to purchase computer hardware and software that even a few years ago would have been prohibitively expensive.

This trend increases the likelihood that small restaurants will be using sophisticated, graphical software and easy-to-use data input devices, including touch screens and hand-held ordering terminals, in the near future. Currently, smaller restaurants are principally purchasing point-of-sale (POS) and front-of-the-house systems to improve customer ordering, speed of service and controls over the sales functions. For roughly $1,000, a POS system yielding excellent management information can be purchased, and $2,000 will buy a system with much greater information-yielding capacity for a one-unit location. Multi-location systems are usually $3,000 to $8,000 per restaurant.

The restaurant owner or operator should research the features of various systems and compare costs closely to determine what system is most appropriate for their operations.

POS systems are designed to improve the placement of customer orders with the kitchen and the invoicing of customers. The system collects the data on all of the day's sales and can be programmed to prepare numerous accounting reports, including breakdowns of sales by server, dining area, meal period and by method of payment (check, cash or credit card). Installing a POS system should improve the quality and quantity of information management has about the restaurants sales and allow them to make better operating decisions.

A POS system or other information hardware and software should be purchased after careful comparison of the features and costs of various systems. Generally, a manufacturer's representative or distributor will be happy to demonstrate the capabilities of their products and discuss their relative merits. When selecting a system, it is best to keep in mind the anticipated growth of the restaurant; although POS systems may be replaced every 6 to 7 years, an operator will want a system that can easily expand along with the restaurant's operations. Ease of use should also be considered; touch screens and hand-held tableside order entry devices are two of the leading-edge technologies that are easy for the waitstaff to use.

While the new technologies may be somewhat intimidating to someone unfamiliar with them, they offer numerous opportunities to reduce costs and improve service and the quantity and quality of management information. A carefully researched purchase is generally a wise investment. For further information and a list of vendors offering restaurant systems, contact the National Restaurant Association Information Service Department, 1200 Seventeenth Street, N.W., Washington D.C. 20036-3097, telephone (202) 331-5900.

# CHAPTER FOUR

# BUDGETING AND BUDGETARY CONTROL

# Introduction

An annual budget is a tool frequently used to assist a restaurant owner or manager in analyzing the restaurant's operating performance. A budget presents the expected revenues and expenses of the restaurant for a future period of time, usually a year. Actual operating results can then be compared against the budget to identify problem areas or trends. Budgets are usually developed on a monthly basis, and then the months are combined to present an annual budget. Monthly budgets allow an operator to measure financial success and identify problems quickly, thereby presenting an opportunity to take corrective actions. The budgeting process allows the restaurant operator to both plan and control his financial results.

The budgeting process varies from company to company; however, some principles are standard.

## The Budgeting Process

The budgeting process should begin with a review of the prior year's budget, assuming one was prepared, and the prior year's actual results to assist in developing reasonable expectations about the coming year. The person most knowledgeable about the restaurant's financial operations is usually the best person to prepare the budget. It is a good idea to enlist the assistance of the restaurant manager, if one is employed, in preparing the budget. This will often motivate the manager to try to achieve the budgeted results.

A worksheet estimating the monthly amounts of each significant revenue and expense item should be developed. These amounts should be estimated based on historical trends and anticipated changes in menu prices, customer counts, number of seats, promotions, food and beverage costs, and other factors influencing the restaurant's performance. These monthly budgeted amounts can then be added together to produce an annual budget. The annual budget is generally presented in the same format as the statement of income.

The proposed budget should be reviewed and approved by the appropriate supervisory personnel or the restaurant owner. Any disagreements in the budget should be resolved and then a final budget approved.

The budgeting process is usually performed during the last two or three months of the restaurant's fiscal year. The more detailed or complex the budgeting is, or the greater the number of properties for which a budget should be developed, the earlier the process should begin.

## Budgetary Control

A budget is of little help to management in running the business if a timely comparison of the actual operating results to the budgeted amounts is not performed. For this reason, preparation of a monthly budget is suggested. After the month's actual operating results have been compared to the budget and differences noted, explanations for significant differences between the two should be sought. Written explanations of these differences are especially helpful if the individual investigating them and the individual to whom the results are ultimately reported are not the same.

Based on the significance of the differences between the actual and budgeted amounts and the reasons for the differences, corrective actions should be considered. The budget will be more useful if it is prepared and analyzed only in the amount of detail that is relevant.

If desired and actual results vary significantly from the budget, the restaurant owner or operator may want to revise the budget at mid-year to make it more useful. Generally, only very significant differences would make this reforecasting worthwhile.

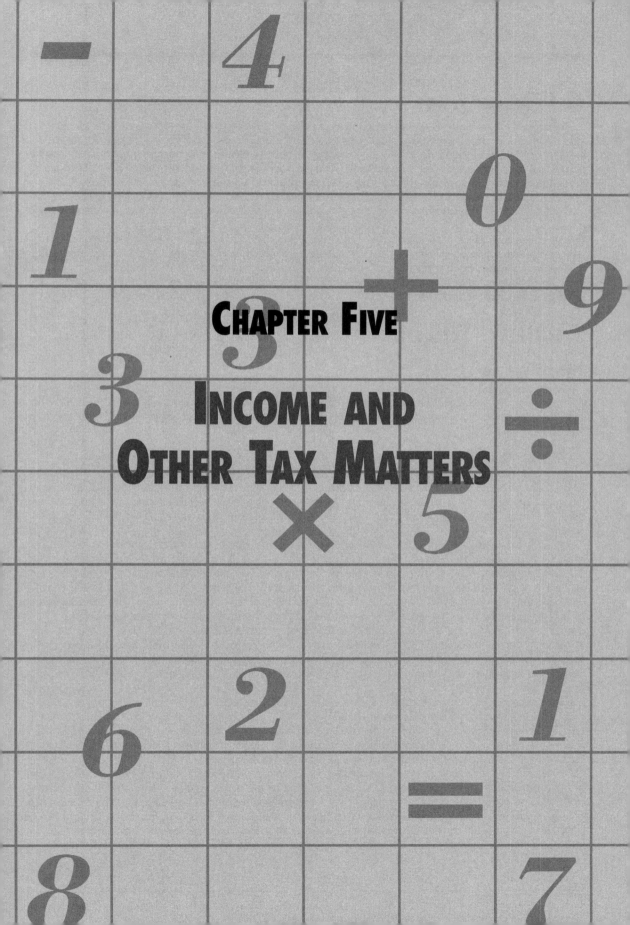

# CHAPTER FIVE

# INCOME AND OTHER TAX MATTERS

# Introduction

Like most other businesses, restaurants are subject to several different types of taxes. These taxes include income taxes, sales and use taxes, property taxes, and payroll taxes. Regardless of the form of the business enterprise (e.g., proprietorship, corporation, partnership, limited liability company, etc.) these taxes are important. This part will include both a general discussion about these taxes and a discussion about several areas that are unique to restaurants.

The topics discussed in this chapter are intended to assist restaurant owners by providing current and accurate information concerning the subject matter covered. However, no assurance is given by the authors or the National Restaurant Association that such information is comprehensive in its coverage of such subject matter or that it is suitable in dealing with a particular problem or business related circumstance. Accordingly, information provided in this chapter should not be relied upon as a substitute for independent research to original sources of authority or consultation with a qualified professional advisor. This chapter does not render any accounting, legal or other professional advice.

# Income Taxes

## Introduction

Most restaurant businesses are subject to federal income tax and, depending upon the state of operation, may be subject to state income tax also. One of the first considerations that may have a significant impact on the amount of income tax a restaurant company pays is the legal form of the operating entity.

### Operating Entity

A restaurant may operate in one of many forms, including a sole proprietorship, corporation (e.g., Subchapter "S" or Chapter "C"), partnership, or in most states a limited liability company (LLC). In addition to the differing levels of legal protection these different forms of doing business give the restaurant owner, the tax consequences to the restaurant owner may also differ significantly.

A sole proprietorship may be used when there is one owner who is a person. When this form of doing business is used, the sole proprietorship itself is not required to file a tax return or pay income taxes. The owner of the sole proprietorship will be responsible for paying the income tax on the net taxable income of the restaurant. The restaurant's income and expenses are reported on Form 1040, Schedule C of the individual owner's tax return. The taxable income of the restaurant shown on Schedule C will be combined with the other components of the owner's taxable income and subject to tax at the applicable individual tax rates.

In addition to income tax, the taxable income of the restaurant operated as a sole proprietorship will be subject to self-employment tax. The self-employment tax rate is the equivalent of the combined employer and employee portions of the social security (FICA) tax. For 1995 the self-employment tax rate is 15.3 percent. This consisted of 12.4 percent for old-age, survivors and disability insurance (OASDI) and 2.9 percent for health insurance (HI). For 1995 OASDI is applied to self-employment income in excess of $400, up to income of $61,200. The 2.9% HI is applied to self-employment income on amounts in excess of $400 with no upper limit. The IRS revises these rates and limits frequently. The self-employment income subject to the tax is first reduced by the taxpayer's wages that are subject to FICA taxes.

A restaurant may be operated as a Chapter C corporation regardless of the number of owners (shareholders). The corporation is also required to file a tax return. Whether or not the taxable income reflected on the corporation's tax return is subject to federal income tax at the corporate level depends on the status of the corporation. If the entity is a C corporation, it is. If the corporation is an S corporation (it has made an election to be taxed under subchapter S of the Internal Revenue Code), it will be taxed for federal purposes in a manner similar to a sole proprietorship or a partnership (i.e., taxable income is taxed only at the owner level, not also at the entity level). An additional significant difference between an S corporation and a sole proprietorship or a partnership relates to self-employment tax. Currently, earnings from an S corporation are not subject to self-employment tax at the owner level. Conversely, earnings from a sole proprietorship or a partnership are subject to self-employment tax at the owner level. However, as of this writing, legislation has been introduced that would also subject S corporation owners to self-employment tax on their distributive share of S corporation taxable income. In addition, the salary paid to an employee-owner of an S corporation is subject to social security taxes.

If a corporation is a C corporation, the net taxable income of the restaurant will be subject to tax at the corporate tax rate. Dividends paid to an individual by a corporation that has not made an S election are not deductible by the corporation and will, generally, be subject to tax at the individual level. Thus, use of a C corporation raises a possibility of a double tax. In addition, the salary paid to an employee-owner of a C corporation is subject to both income and social security taxes.

A partnership may be used when there are two or more owners. The owners may be any type of entity (e.g., person, corporation, partnership, trust, etc.). Although the partnership is required to file a tax return, its taxable income is not subject to tax at the partnership level. The taxable income is divided among the partners of the partnership according to each partner's respective ownership percentage. The tax liability for each partner's respective share of the taxable income is computed based on the tax law applicable to that respective partner. For partners who are individuals, the tax treatment of their distributive share of partnership taxable income is subject to the same rules as that of a sole proprietor, with the exception of the form on which it is reported. For partners who are corporations, the tax treatment of their distributive share of partnership taxable income is subject to the rules discussed in the preceding paragraphs. Many times a partnership will make a cash distribution to the partners to enable them to pay the tax liability associated with their respective share of partnership taxable income. These distributions generally are tax free to the partner.

The LLC is a new form of doing business. The LLC offers the limited liability of a corporation while providing the tax benefits of a partnership. As of this writing, 47 states and the District of Columbia have adopted LLC statutes. Hawaii, Massachusetts, and Vermont have LLC statutes pending. In the last two years, there has been a rapid increase in Internal Revenue Service rulings approving LLCs as taxable as partnerships, provided they meet certain requirements when they are formed. LLCs offer limited liability, greater flexibility than a limited partnership or S corporation, and treatment as a partnership for tax purposes so that all of the income, deductions, credits, gains, and losses flow through to the owners.

A business may not automatically choose to do business as an LLC. In addition to meeting the partnership requirements of the Internal Revenue Code, the business must file with a state and meet that particular state's requirements for organization. LLC statutes may vary from state to state. Thus, it is very important to understand the state statute under which your LLC will be governed.

As of this writing, the top federal tax rate for a C corporation is 35 percent while the top rate for an individual is 39.6 percent. As you can see, determining the type of entity to use for your restaurant operation is a complex matter with significant tax implications. There is not one right answer for all situations. Your attorney and your tax advisor can assist you in determining which form will work to your best advantage.

## Depreciation and Amortization

The tax law permits a depreciation deduction for the exhaustion, wear and tear of property used in a trade or business, or of property held for the production of income. Depreciation is not allowable for property used for personal purposes, such as a residence or an automobile used solely for pleasure.

Depreciation is allowable for tangible property, but not for inventories, stock in trade, land apart from its improvements, or a depletable natural resource. An intangible asset such as a patent, copyright, license, franchise, contract, favorable leasehold, or similar asset is amortizable. In some cases, goodwill is also amortizable.

The methods of depreciation are dependent on when the property was place in service. The Modified Accelerated Cost Recovery System (MACRS) generally applies to tangible property placed in service after 1986 and the Accelerated Cost Recovery System (ACRS) applies to property placed in service after 1980 and before 1987. Under MACRS and ACRS, the cost or other basis of property is recovered over the recovery period (life assigned by the law) for the asset. For assets placed in service before 1981 and assets that are excluded from MACRS and ACRS (such as intangible property placed into service prior to the effective date of the Revenue Reconciliation Act of 1993) special rules apply.

The depreciation and amortization rules govern how fast a business can write off the cost of assets. The IRS has published tables that are to be used to determine the recovery period of an asset subject to MACRS depreciation. These tables establish the correct recovery period. A separate asset class exists for distributive trades and services including restaurants. For specific rules related to the calculation of depreciation, refer to IRS publication 534, *Depreciation*, and publication 334, *Tax Guide for Small Business*.

Special rules apply to intangible assets. You should contact your tax advisor for assistance in determining whether or not you are entitled to a tax deduction for amortization of your intangible assets.

Many states have their own rules which are different from the federal rules described.

## Election to Expense Certain Depreciable Business Assets

Rather than capitalizing and depreciating certain property, a taxpayer may, subject to certain limitations, elect to treat up to $17,500 of the cost of the property as an expense. Generally, the type of property qualifying for this election is tangible personal property.

The depreciable basis of property for which this election is made must be reduced by the amount of the expense.

### Example

In 19X5, XYZ company purchased a piece of equipment for $50,000. Assuming XYZ is not subject to the applicable limitations, they may elect to expense $17,500 of the equipment cost in 19X5. The remaining $32,500 ($50,000–$17,500) depreciable basis of the equipment will be depreciated over its useful life beginning in 19X5.

For limitations related to this expensing election, consult your tax advisor.

## Tips

### IRS Forms Required to Be Filed

As of this writing, the following forms are required to be filed by the employer or employee with respect to tip income:

1. **Form 4070, Employee's Report of Tips to Employer.** This form is required to be filed by employee's receiving tips of $20 or more in a month while working for any one employer. Employees are required to provide their employer with this form no later than the 10th day of the next month. If the 10th day falls on a Saturday, Sunday or legal holiday, the report may be provided to the employer on the next day that is not a Saturday, Sunday or legal holiday.
2. **Form 4137, Social Security Tax on Unreported Tip Income.** This form is to be used by employees who did not report all of their tips to their employer or if their Form(s) W-2 shows allocated tips that must be reported as income. The purpose of the form is to compute social security and Medicare tax owed on the unreported tips. Employees include this form with their form 1040.
3. **Form 8027, Employer Annual Information Return of Tip Income and Allocated Tips.** Form 8027 is used by large food or beverage establishments when the employer is required to make annual reports to the IRS on receipts from food or beverage operations and tips reported by employees. As defined by the IRS, a large food or beverage establishment is one to which all of the following apply:

- Food or beverage is provided for consumption on the premises.
- Tipping is a customary practice.
- More than 10 employees were normally employed on a typical business day during the preceding calendar year.

IRS publications 937, Employment Taxes and Information Returns, and 531, Reporting Tip Income, provide additional information regarding your filing requirements as an employer. You should consult your tax advisor regarding your specific filing requirements.

## Internal Revenue Service's Tip Audits

A common problem employers experience in the restaurant industry is the underreporting of tip income by the restaurant employees. This became a significant problem for restaurateurs with the enactment of OBRA '87 when employers became liable to pay FICA on unreported as well as reported tips. The Fair Labor Standards Act compounds this problem by preventing an employer from reporting tips on behalf of an employee.

Recently, the IRS has been paying special attention to tip reporting and the payment of employer FICA related thereto. The methods that the IRS has adopted in performing tip audits have generated significant controversy between the IRS and restaurateurs. Additionally, the IRS found the traditional approach, that is, auditing the restaurants and the waiters and waitresses after the returns were filed, wasn't correcting the problem. Forms 8027, Employers Annual Information Return of Tip Income and Allocated Tips, often show more charged tips than the total tips reported by the waiters and waitresses. The IRS has decided to try to assure greater compliance by dealing with the issue before future returns are filed.

In an attempt to alleviate the problems associated with underreported tip income and underreported FICA taxes on tips, the IRS has established two programs. The first program established by the IRS was a National Tip Rate Determination/Education Program, which involves mutual agreements between restaurant owners and IRS district directors regarding the rate of tip income reported by the tipped employees.

Under this program, the IRS contacts restaurants and offers them a tip agreement (TRDA). If the restaurants can get 75 percent of their waiters and waitresses to sign an agreement to report the correct amount of tips (as worked out by the IRS), the IRS will agree not to audit the restaurants or their tipped employees on the tip issue as long as they are in compliance with the agreement. The IRS plans to monitor compliance with the tip agreements through the information contained on Forms 8027. The effect on the restaurants—the increased FICA taxes on the tips—may be offset by a credit against the employer's income tax liability. This credit is discussed in the next section.

As a direct result of objections raised by members of the foodservice industry to TRDA, an alternative program was developed. The alternative program is called the Tip Reporting Alternative Commitment, or TRAC, a pro forma agreement that the IRS will enter into with participating food and beverage service employers. TRAC is available as an alternative to TRDA. The IRS has indicated it will permit all eligible employers to enter into TRAC agreements.

Under a TRAC agreement, employers agree to establish procedures to ensure accurate tip reporting by their employees; maintain quarterly educational programs to train newly hired employees and update existing employees regarding their tip reporting obligations; and comply with all Federal tax requirements for filing returns, paying and depositing taxes, and maintaining records. In turn, the IRS agrees, with certain exceptions, to demand the employer's share of FICA taxes on employees' tip income solely on the amounts reported on Forms 4137, Social Security and Medicare Tax on Unreported Tip Income, filed by employees with their Forms 1040; or Forms 885-T, Adjustment of Social Security Tax on Tip Income Not Reported to Employer, prepared at the conclusion of employees tip examinations.

You should note that tip reporting continues to be a controversial matter between restaurateurs and the IRS. Accordingly, it is an area subject to change. The preceding information regarding tip reporting is current as of the writing of this book. However, you should consult your tax advisor for subsequent developments.

### FICA Tax Credit

Most of the public attention directed to the Omnibus Budget Reconciliation Act of 1993 (OBRA '93) concerned the tax increases. However, one provision added at the last minute provides substantial tax relief to restaurants in the form of a business credit for employer social security taxes paid on employee cash tips. Employees who receive tips must report them to their employer. The employer is required to treat these reported tips as compensation, and must withhold FICA tax from the employee and pay the employer share. If the wages paid by the restaurant are less than the required minimum wage, some or all of the reported tip income can be applied to bring wages up to that minimum.

OBRA '93 gives restaurants a business tax credit for the *employer's* share of the FICA tax they are required to pay on reported tips in excess of those used to meet the minimum wage requirements. This credit can be used to reduce the restaurant's income tax liability. There is no credit for the employee's FICA tax liability. This provision does not apply to other employers that may have tipped employees, only to food and beverage establishments.

# Sales and Use Taxes

## Introduction

Currently, 46 states and the District of Columbia have adopted some form of sales tax. In general, sales tax is imposed on the sale of tangible property either directly at the time of sale or measured by sales. The seller is responsible for the tax and is entitled to recover the tax from its customers. Taxes that are imposed directly on the sale are commonly referred to as "consumer sales taxes" because the tax is based on the sales price and is paid by the consumer.

A complement to a states sales tax is the use tax. A use tax is imposed on the storage, use, or other consumption of tangible property in the state. Responsibility for the use tax falls on the consumer and is intended to tax those who purchase property from an out-of-state vendor. The use tax is intended to give in-state retailers the ability to compete on price with out-of-state competitors.

Many of the states that have adopted sales and use taxes have also adopted legislation that permits cities and counties to enact their own sales and use taxes.

Generally, the state taxing authorities require sales and use tax returns to be filed either monthly or quarterly. Some states, however, allow taxpayers to file annual returns. In addition, states may require estimated tax payments for quarterly or annual filers. For further information on state and local sales and use taxes, contact your tax advisor.

## Exemptions

Many of the states that have adopted sales and use taxes provide exemptions from the tax for certain types of sales transactions and on the sale of certain types of property. The most common exemption from sales and use tax is for the purchase of tangible property for resale. Although purchase for resale is a common transaction, sellers and purchasers should carefully structure and document each transaction to meet the requirements for exemption in the state of purchase and the state of use or resale.

In addition to purchase for resale, many states provide an exemption on the sale of specific types of tangible property. Some of the more common exemptions are for the sale of prescription drugs, medical devices and food products. You should note, however, that states vary widely in their definition and taxation of property. The sales or use tax implications should be reviewed on a state by state basis.

Generally, transactions involving the purchase of tangible property for use in a state or the sale of tangible property in a state are subject to tax unless otherwise exempted. With this basic presumption, sales and use tax matters can be identified and resolved before they become an issue under audit. In the following discussion some of the more common sales and use tax issues, as they relate to the foodservice industry, are identified.

## Purchase for Resale

As previously noted, one of the more common exemptions from sales and use tax is on the purchase of tangible property for resale. In the foodservice industry, however, determining what constitutes a purchase for resale can cause some controversy. In general, items of a nonreusable nature furnished with a meal are considered to be sold with the meal. Accordingly, such items are considered purchased for resale and exempt from sales or use tax. Examples of such non-reusable items would include products such as straws, paper napkins and toothpicks. Suppliers of these products should require resale certificates to support and document this type of exemption.

## Sales Subject to Tax

Many states provide an exemption for the sale of food products at retail by grocery stores, supermarkets, and convenience stores. However, the majority of states tax the sale of food products sold as meals or in a form consumable by the customer at the time of sale.

In general, sales tax applies on the sale of meals or hot prepared food products furnished by restaurants, hotels and concessionaires for consumption at the seller's place of business. In addition, tax may also apply on the sale of some or all take-out or to-go orders. For example, in California, the sale of all hot prepared food products is taxable whether sold for immediate consumption or to-go. Also, cold food products may be taxable if suitable for immediate consumption. Sales tax may also apply on mandatory gratuities, banquet room charges and service charges in connection with the sale of meals. Issues may also exist around the taxability of employee meals. Since states vary widely in their definition and treatment of these matters, you should consult your tax advisor for further assistance in this area.

In addition to the sale of meals and food products, restaurants may also sell alcoholic beverages. In general, alcoholic beverages are sold "tax included," which means the stated price being charged includes the appropriate sales tax. State auditors are likely to review a taxpayer's method of collecting and reporting tax on these sales.

## Use Tax Accruals

Use taxes have become increasingly popular with state taxing authorities in recent years. Use tax liability arises from the purchase of supplies and equipment from out-of-state vendors for use in the purchaser's state. Use tax also applies on self-consumed property held for resale (i.e.: free meals, complementary drinks, waste, etc.). Many businesses are unaware of the potential for exposure until it is too late and an auditor has assessed tax, interest and penalties on the underpayment.

To avoid the additional cost of interest and penalties, you should pay use tax with your sales tax report. To do this, review your invoices from the purchase of supplies and equipment from out-of-state vendors. Pay use tax based on the cost of property reflected on the invoice that is subject to sales or use tax in your state. Consult your tax advisor to determine what property is taxable in your state.

# Property Taxes

In addition to the majority of states that impose property taxes, many local jurisdictions, such as counties, impose property taxes as well. Since foodservice is a capital intensive industry, property taxes also can be a significant part of a restaurant company's operating expenses.

## Real Property Tax

In 1993, approximately $193 billion in property taxes was collected in the U.S., an amount that exceeded both personal and corporate income taxes. For many taxpayers in the foodservice industry, real property tax represents a significant portion of their operating costs. Therefore, accurate representation of property values in local tax jurisdictions is critical.

In most jurisdictions, the owners of real property are taxed based on the assessed value of the property and the appropriate tax rate. Real property includes all types of property including single family dwellings, offices, industrial property, retail property and hotels. In most states, the basis for the assessed value is fair market value. The concept of fair market value is fundamental to the assessment of real estate; however, valuation for local assessing authorities differs in both scope and methodology from traditional appraisal services. In states where the fair market value concept is in place, you should be aware that assessed values are influenced by the same general factors that influence the value of real estate overall. These factors include industry condition, the business cycle, demographics, and supply and demand.

You should be familiar with the tax cycle in your respective state. Although property tax cycles and the basis for assessments vary from state to state, there are some common denominators that you should be aware of. Typically, taxes are due once per year and are payable in multiple installments. In the event the taxpayer disagrees with the assessed value, he may appeal. Filing an appeal challenges the current property tax assessment. You must protect your administrative right by filing an assessment appeal with the assessment authority. An appeal should be filed in cases where the assessed value exceeds fair market value. Although informal methods may be used when approaching the local assessor's office to discuss reductions, you may lose the ability to challenge the assessment formally unless an appeal is filed in a timely manner.

In most states the affected party has the right to appeal the value of the property. The affected party ultimately is the individual/corporation who pays the taxes. In many lease structures, the tenant (lessee) has ultimate responsibility for the payment of property tax.

You should also understand the requirements of the appeal process in the states in which you do business. In some states, taxing authorities may reassess the value of real property at any time. However, in other states the value of real property can only be reassessed upon the occurrence of a specific event. For example, in California, the value of real property can only be reassessed when a change of ownership occurs. Certain states require state certified general appraisers and/or attorneys to testify at assessment appeal hearings. Additionally, in most jurisdictions, the equalization process assumes that the county assessor has properly assessed the property and the burden of proof is on the taxpayer.

Real property taxes are a fixed expenditure for many businesses in the foodservice industry. By using the appeal process, real property tax expense can be controlled in instances where the assessed value exceeds fair market value. You should consult your local tax advisor for assistance with the appeal process.

## Personal Property Tax

Personal or business property, by definition, is all property other than real estate that is not exempt by local taxing authorities. Many states impose a property tax on personal property used in a trade or business and assess based on a valuation of that property. Generally, states require taxpayers to report personal property by filing annual returns for each business location within a local taxing jurisdiction. Returns can include the cost of all machinery, equipment, furnishings, improvements (tenant), etc, classified by asset type and summarized by year of acquisition. In addition, some states may require reporting inventory held for sale that is typically on hand. Returns are subject to audit in most states on a periodic cycle of either three or four years.

Similar to real property assessments, personal property is assessed on an assessment date. The significance of the assessment date is that the assessment is based on property owned or on location on that date. For example, if the assessment date is January 1, 1996, the purchase of equipment items on December 31, 1995 will be fully taxable. If that same equipment is purchased on January 2, 1996, there will be no property tax on those purchases until the next assessment date of January 1, 1997.

Some assessing authorities apply a factor to the reported costs to derive an assessable value. This factor is based on that taxing authority's determination of an appropriate life for each type of equipment. This life is not related to the life assigned for financial statement purposes nor to the life used for income tax purposes. This process causes the property tax base of an asset to decrease each year.

When reporting personal property, taxpayers in most taxing jurisdictions are required to classify the assets on the return. Each category of assets is assigned a life based upon its classification. The property tax is based on the return, therefore, classification of the assets in correct categories is extremely important. The shorter the life of the property, the less property tax you will pay over the life of the property. For example, incorrectly classifying computer equipment as general machinery and equipment may cause it to be taxed too high (e.g., as a 15-year vs. 5-year life asset). Classification of personal property will vary by county or state.

Classification of property as real or personal also varies by county or state. Many items of personal property become permanently affixed to real property. Such costs may be incorrectly taxed twice: once as real property and once as personal property, depending on how they are reported by the taxpayer and assessed by the assessor. Typical situations in which double taxation may occur include remodeling, tenant improvements and/or repairs, signs, and walk-in cooler and freezer costs.

Personal property assessed to restaurant owners/operators may include the following equipment categories: kitchen equipment and improvements, dining room furniture and improvements, smallwares (china, glassware, flatware), hot and cold self serve bars (stand alone islands), inter-office equipment, and construction-in-progress. Common ways to consistently reduce personal property tax are to:

- Report the above categories on attached spreadsheets, not necessarily on provided forms;
- Accurately report only those assets that are present on the assessment date and prepare an audit trail when deviating from the books and records;
- Identify equipment that is obsolete because of new lines or types of state-of-the-art technology;
- Review improvement costs and defer reporting costs of items replaced through remodeling, repair and maintenance, etc.;
- Report supplies (and inventory, when applicable to that state) that are not part of the final food product (either eat-in or take-out), distinguish and avoid reporting smallwares already capitalized as kitchen equipment, and report a level of supplies that are on-hand and not year-end totals

You should consult your tax advisor for additional information regarding the personal property tax requirements for the taxing jurisdictions in which you operate.

# Payroll Taxes

An employer is required to withhold federal and state income taxes on all wages paid to an employee. Generally, an employer is the person for whom one or more individuals perform services as an employee. Individuals qualify as employees when they are subject to the will and control of the person for whom they are performing services, with respect to both how and what they do.

Employers must withhold federal and state income taxes and FICA (social security and Medicare) taxes. As these are withheld, they are not an expense of the employer. Employers must pay a matching amount of FICA tax plus federal and state unemployment taxes. These are all paid at the employer's expense. Some states, such as California, also require the withholding of state disability taxes. All withholding taxes are deducted from each employee's gross pay to determine the net paycheck. Payroll taxes withheld plus the employer's share of payroll tax expense must be deposited with the federal and state governments on a regular basis. The timing is determined by the amount of payroll tax due.

## Wages

For payroll tax purposes, wages include hourly wages, annual salaries, commissions, bonuses, piece rates, distribution of profits and incentive payments. Cash tips are also considered wages even though they are paid by the customer. For federal purposes, tips are only considered for payroll tax purposes when they are at least $20 per employee in a calendar month.

## Withholding Taxes

At the start of employment, each employee must complete and sign Form W-4, Employee's Withholding Allowance Certificate. This form tells the employer the filing status (generally, the marital status), and the number of exemptions the employee is claiming. This information is used to properly calculate the employee's income tax withholding.

Federal income tax withholding is calculated by using special withholding tables the IRS provides in their annual "Circular E." Most states have similar methods of determining withholding; however, some use a percentage of the federal tax or some other method. FICA tax is made up of a combination of OASDI tax at 6.2% on a maximum annual wage of $61,200, plus 1.45% on all taxable wages. The FICA rate changes periodically, with the wage limit changing annually. These are the current rates and limits for 1995. The employer calculates FICA and withholds this from the employee's check. Under the matching provision, the employer generally must remit 15.5% when depositing payroll taxes, 7.65% withheld from the employee, and another 7.65% of employer expense.

In general, states do not have withholding similar to FICA. However, some states have state disability insurance withholding, which is calculated as a fixed percentage on a certain wage limit.

The other major payroll taxes are unemployment insurance, both federal and state. These are the employer's expense. Federal unemployment insurance, or FUTA, is paid at the rate of .8% (.008) on the first $7,000 of each employees wages per year. Each state has its own system for establishing an unemployment insurance tax rate, but the states generally set a certain wage limit. Most states base the rate on a unique employer's experience. A new employer is assigned a set rate, but then deposits made by the employer are set up in an account and tracked separately. Payments to terminated employees reduce this account. The balance is then evaluated periodically to revise the employer's unemployment insurance tax rate. Whenever there is a wage limit for payroll tax purposes, this limit applies to the current employer only. If an employee changes jobs during the year, this limit starts over with each new employer.

## Policies and Procedures

Federal taxes must be deposited frequently. The schedule depends on the amount of tax due. The tax must be paid to an authorized financial institution. Most states have a similar deposit requirement; however, the payment is usually mailed to the state taxing authority.

The federal deposit includes income tax withheld and FICA taxes, while the state deposit includes state income tax withheld, unemployment insurance, and disability taxes, if any. FUTA taxes must be deposited quarterly, if the tax due exceeds $100.

Federal Form 941 must be filed quarterly to report all wages paid and payroll taxes due or paid. Most states have a similar form and filing requirement. Annually, federal Form 940 must be filed to report federal unemployment tax. Also, W-2 forms must be prepared and filed annually with the IRS and each state. A copy must also be provided to the employee. W-2 forms are submitted with a Form W-3 transmittal form to the Social Security Administration. Each state also has a transmittal form.

For specific information regarding your state payroll tax requirements, contact your local tax advisor.

# CHAPTER SIX

# RESTAURANT CONTROLS

# Introduction

Restaurant operations are logically divisible into four basic elements:  cost of merchandise purchased for resale; salaries and wages, including employee benefits; operating expenses; and net income.

The first two elements can be divided into three major cost categories: food cost, beverage cost, and salaries and wages. These three costs, combined into what is sometimes known as "prime cost," typically consume between 60 and 70% of the restaurant sales dollar while operating expenses and net income represent the balance.

The object of control procedures is to provide a flow of information on those variable costs and expenses which management can influence through professional management techniques. Although operating and other expenses are partly variable, many are fixed and the overall share of the income dollar is relatively small. Therefore, controls should be put in place for food and beverage costs and payroll expenses because they represent the largest controllable cost elements.

The purpose of this section is to suggest controls over these three major cost elements, and illustrations are included. However, each restaurant operation has different requirements, and controls should be developed and modified to meet individual needs.

# Food Cost Control

This section is written primarily for the restaurant operator who is not in a position to maintain any extensive food control system and yet desires to know what the food costs are from day to day. Many restaurant operators find it cost-effective to use existing employees and train them as part-time control clerks. It may be possible to use existing office staff to perform and follow these control functions based on a system designed to meet their requirements. The simplified systems and reporting forms illustrated in this section can be part of a larger or more sophisticated system. It would not be practical to describe these controls in detail in this text. It is advisable that professional help be obtained in setting up and using the more detailed and elaborate control systems.

An understanding of the importance of proper purchasing, receiving, storing, preparation and production control is essential to the effective use of control procedures. A management evaluation of these functions should precede any consideration for establishing controls.

No control system has yet been devised which, by means of the paperwork alone, will bring about the desired results. Food control is not only a clerical function, but it also calls for close attention on the part of management and food-handling employees to execute the proper procedures of purchasing, receiving, storing and preparation. Daily cost figures generated by a food-control system serve as a guide to those in charge and enable them to base corrective steps on factual data.

## Purchasing

Stated simply, efficient purchasing is obtaining the quality of merchandise desired at the most favorable price. To accomplish this it is necessary to know the grade, size, weight, pack and quality of food most suitable to the particular restaurant operation.  Competitive bids are advisable where the restaurant operator is in a position to obtain them.

In some respects, the food purchasing process has been made less complex with the availability of so many preportioned and prefabricated foods. Food processed this way also requires that purchase specifications be established since sizes, weights and quality vary widely.

## Receiving

Proper checking of the quality, weight and count of merchandise when it is delivered is probably the most frequently ignored of all of the rules of good control, and yet it is most important.

If it is at all possible, the authority to receive merchandise should be limited to one trustworthy person. It is not good business to allow anyone in the kitchen to sign for deliveries or to permit the delivery of merchandise directly to the stock room or coolers without first checking it in. Both of these circumstances invite losses and increase costs.

The control of merchandise is much more efficient if a daily receiving record is kept on all deliveries and if requisition forms are used for all goods withdrawn from the storeroom. These records can be obtained at most hotel and restaurant stationers, who carry them in stock form.

The type of scale used is important. It should have a graduated dial or other indicator accurate to the half-pound or 0.25 kilograms. Errors of as little as one pound can be considerable at the high unit cost of some food.

## Storing

Merchandise should be stored promptly after it is accepted. The storage areas should be kept clean and orderly. Old merchandise should be dated and moved to the front so that the "first-in, first-out" practice can be followed.

The temperatures of the coolers should be checked frequently to protect the contents. Locks should be provided for all storage areas.

Inventories should be taken at each month-end. A bound split-leaf inventory book which provides for twelve consecutive inventories with a single listing of the items is recommended for foods stored on the same shelf in the same location each month. For foods stored in refrigerators, freezers, and reach-in refrigerators and kitchen areas, it is best to write the inventory as taken. There are, of course, many instances where a preprinted inventory book or sheets can be used throughout the restaurant.

## Preparation

Merchandise should be prepared in moderate quantities and as near to the time it is to be served as possible. Advance preparation not only results in deterioration in the quality and appearance of the products, but also may cause substantial direct losses. Recipes should be established and used to sustain quality and maintain a consistent cost.

## Production Control

The quantities of the various menu items to be prepared should be based on advance forecasting of quantities which in turn is based on the history of the number of items sold. Many restaurants with fixed menus can plan production schedules with considerable accuracy. The favorable execution of this process saves on food cost by reducing waste caused by leftover food or by eliminating shrinkage.

Production of certain high-cost entrees should be controlled by means of a daily inventory or sales report which compares production with actual sales.

## Control Procedures

In the case of a small restaurant where there is no storeroom to control, and where the operator does not use a receiving sheet or requisitions, a very simple daily summary of sales and costs may be enough as a guide to food costs. This information can be placed on a columnar sheet with a line for each day's transactions as illustrated in the following form:

| Date | Sales | | Food Purchases | | Food Cost Ratio | |
|---|---|---|---|---|---|---|
| | Today | To-Date | Today | To-Date | Today | To-Date |
| | $ | $ | $ | $ | % | % |
| 2 | | | | | | |
| 3 | | | | | | |
| 4 | | | | | | |
| 5 | | | | | | |
| 6 | | | | | | |
| | | | | | | |
| 29 | | | | | | |
| 30 | | | | | | |
| 31 | | | | | | |
| Monthly Total $_____ | | | $ | | % | % |
| Add Beginning Inventory | | | | | | |
| Total | | | | | | |
| Less Ending Inventory | | | | | | |
| Net Cost of Food for the | | | $_____ | | | |
| Month | | | | | | _____% |

It is obvious in situations where daily purchases are considered at cost that the ratio of cost to sales may fluctuate from day to day. However, the cumulative cost ratio becomes a fairly accurate barometer, provided that the food inventory is maintained at a reasonably uniform level. Sales data come either from the daily report or from cash register tapes. The purchases come either from a receiving record, where all invoices are recorded, or directly from invoices which have been totaled for the day.

The use of requisitions for supplies taken from the storeroom and storeroom refrigerators is the most exact method of recording costs. Effective use of requisitions requires training and supervision of production and storeroom personnel. It also requires a well-designed storeroom which contains not only dry goods but also storage refrigerators. Requisitioning functions smoothly from a properly designed storeroom. It is difficult to requisition from refrigerators located in a working kitchen.

Advantages of requisitioning are that production staff are forced to plan ahead and the food cost is more exact. These factors make requisitioning the most accurate basis for a system of control; therefore, requisitions for supplies from the storeroom should be mandatory if the storage areas are effectively designed.

It is usually necessary to charge out certain items as they are purchased. These are referred to as direct purchases and include any merchandise that must be delivered immediately to the preparation department. The extent of such direct purchases depends largely on the design of the storeroom and the location of the refrigerators. If these are in the kitchen, it is likely that all food except staple items would be charged directly to operations when purchased.

If a receiving record and requisitions (for items issued from a food storeroom) are used, a columnar sheet like the summary of food costs and sales, Form 7, is recommended as a simplified daily control.

The use of this form requires that a receiving record be maintained, whereby separate totals of purchases charged to the storeroom and direct charges to the kitchen are provided. It also requires the use of requisitions for withdrawals from the storeroom. These must be cost-priced, extended and totaled. The use of the columns on Form 7, included in this section, are explained by column number at the bottom of the form.

The fluctuation in the to-date food-cost ratio is used as an indication of the efficiency of the restaurant operation. The immediate investigation of the causes for any unusual increase in that figure often brings about prompt correction and improved results.

## Summary of Food Cost and Sales

For Month of _____, Year

| Date | (1) Store-room Inventory at Beginning | + (2) Store-room Purchases | = (3) Total | + (4) Store-room Issues | (5) Direct Purchases | = (6) Total Cost | - (7) Deduct Transfers to Beverage | = (8) Net Food Cost Today | (9) Net Food Cost To-Date | (10) Food Sales Today | (11) Food Sales To-Date | (12) Cost Ratio to Sales Today | (13) Cost Ratio to Sales To-Date |
|---|---|---|---|---|---|---|---|---|---|---|---|---|---|
| 1 | | | | | | | | | | | | | |
| 2 | | | | | | | | | | | | | |
| 3 | | | | | | | | | | | | | |
| 28 | | | | | | | | | | | | | |
| 29 | | | | | | | | | | | | | |
| 30 | | | | | | | | | | | | | |
| TOTALS | | | | | | | | | | | | | |

Explanation of Columns:
Column 1 + 2 = 3
Column 3 - 4 = 1
Column 4 + 5 = 6
Column 6 - 7 = 8

Column 9 = Cumulative of Column 8
Column 11 = Cumulative of Column 10
Column 12 = 8 ÷ 10
Column 13 = 9 ÷ 11

# Analysis of Food Purchases

Some restaurant operators want to go further into analyzing their costs and do so by classifying their purchases into major groups or categories. The individual group cost ratios to sales can then be easily determined.

The following illustrates three such methods of classification in varying degree of detail.

| Classification A | | Classification B | | Classification C | |
|---|---|---|---|---|---|
| Number | Item | Number | Item | Number | Item |
| 1. | Meats and Poultry | 1. | Meats | 1. | Beef Strip |
| | | | | 2. | Beef Filet |
| | | | | 3. | Beef Other |
| | | | | 4. | Veal |
| | | | | 5. | Lamb |
| | | | | 6. | Pork and Pork Provisions |
| | | 2. | Poultry | 7. | Poultry |
| 2. | Fish | 3. | Fish | 8. | Seafood |
| 3. | Produce | 4. | Vegetables | 9. | Vegetables |
| 4. | Staples | | | 10. | Salads and Relishes |
| | | 5. | Fruits | 11. | Fruits |
| | | 6. | Staples | 12. | Eggs |
| | | | | 13. | Cheese |
| | | 7. | Butter | 14. | Butter |
| | | | | 15. | Shortening and Oil |
| | | | | 16. | Coffee and Tea |
| | | | | 17. | Staples |
| 5. | Milk and Cream | 8. | Milk and Cream | 18. | Milk and Cream |
| 6. | Bread and Rolls | 9. | Bakery | 19. | Bakery and Pastry |
| 7. | Ice Cream | 10. | Ice Cream | 20. | Ice Cream |

The three illustrations of how food purchases might be classified show that the extent of the analysis of purchases depends on the judgment of the restaurant operator and the value that the detail compiled may have to the particular restaurant. Classification C is the preferred grouping and takes more effort to prepare than A or B groupings.

Form 8 is a combination daily receiving and food purchase distribution report. The form illustrated covers a minimum number of food classifications. Expansion is accomplished by simply adding the required number of columns.

In using this form, each invoice should be identified by vendor's name, number and total amount. The amount of each invoice should then be distributed according to the categories listed in the columnar headings, and the various categories should be totaled. If non-food items are invoiced with food, a column must be added to separate the non-food purchases.

## Food Receiving and Distribution Record

Day _____

Date _____

Sales Today _____

Sales to Date _____

| Vendor | (1) Invoice# | (2) Total Invoice | (3) Beef | (4) Other Meats Poultry | (5) Seafood | (6) Produce | (7) Staples | (8) Dairy | (9) Bread Rolls |
|---|---|---|---|---|---|---|---|---|---|
| | | | | | | | | | |
| | | | | | | | | | |
| | | | | | | | | | |
| | | | | | | | | | |
| | | | | | | | | | |
| | | | | | | | | | |
| | | | | | | | | | |
| | | | | | | | | | |
| | | | | | | | | | |
| | | | | | | | | | |
| | | | | | | | | | |
| | | | | | | | | | |
| | | | | | | | | | |
| | | | | | | | | | |
| | | | | | | | | | |
| | | | | | | | | | |
| | | | | | | | | | |
| | | | | | | | | | |
| | | | | | | | | | |
| Total Purchase Today | | | | | | | | | |
| Less: Transfers to Bar | | | | | | | | | |
| Total Cost Today | | | | | | | | | |
| Total Cost To-Date | | | | | | | | | |
| Cost Percentage To-Date | | | | | | | | | |

Explanation of columns:
Column 2 = Column 3 to 9

Once all purchases have been totaled and decreased by the value of possible transfers to bar, the total cost for the day is shown under the total invoice heading. When this total is established, the cost (purchase) components should also be shown under the applicable commodity-cost totals. They should be balanced to the previously established total purchase cost of the day.

By adding the "today" cost figures in all columns to those recorded for the preceding day or days, the total cost to-date is established.

By dividing the "total" cost, as well as all its component costs, by the sales figures for the corresponding period, the overall food-cost percentage, as well as the various component commodity-cost ratios, will be known.

If the total food-cost ratio increases, that increase will be reflected in one or more of the commodity-cost ratios shown in the distribution. This will indicate where attention should be directed and corrective action taken.

In many restaurants, several sheets of the food receiving and distribution record may be required, thus making its use for convenient study a little awkward. Also, since the form is a combination receiving record, it may be used often by several persons. For these reasons and others, it may be practical for a purchase analysis of this type to use a four-column report similar to Form 9, which accumulates data and shows ratios. The report can be made weekly, bimonthly or monthly. Comparisons can be made to a budgeted amount, to the same period last month, to the year-to-date costs last year or to any other appropriate category.

The first two columns show the distribution of purchases for the current period and last period. The second two columns show the ratio of each item to food sales for the current period and for the previous period.

# Food Purchases by Commodity Classification

Date _____

Period Covered _____

Sales for Period _____

| Food Classification | Amount | | Ratios | |
|---|---|---|---|---|
| | This Period | Last Period | This Period | Last Period |
| Beef Strip | | | | |
| Beef Fillet | | | | |
| Beef Other | | | | |
| Veal | | | | |
| Lamb | | | | |
| Pork and Provisions | | | | |
| Poultry | | | | |
| Seafood | | | | |
| Vegetables | | | | |
| Salads and Relishes | | | | |
| Fruit | | | | |
| Eggs | | | | |
| Butter | | | | |
| Shortening and Oil | | | | |
| Coffee and Tea | | | | |
| Groceries and Staples | | | | |
| Milk and Cream | | | | |
| Bakery and Pastry | | | | |
| Ice Cream | | | | |
| Total | | | | |

Comments: _____

# Beverage Cost Control

Beverage cost makes up a share of total cost of goods sold in varying amounts, depending on the type of bar operation and the volume of sales. Because the gross margin is far greater for beverage than for food, each point by which beverage cost is reduced translates into a higher proportion of gross profit. For these and other reasons the restaurant operator should know what the beverage-cost ratio is from day to day or from week to week. The control of beverage can best be accomplished by setting up a separate control on the stockrooms and a separate control on the bars.

## Beverage Stock Room

The stockroom, or storeroom, should be kept securely locked at all times, and only one person should have access to it for the purpose of storing and issuing the beverage. Requisitions should be required for all merchandise issued. These should be written in duplicate so that the bottles issued can be checked by the bartender against the copy.

## Bar Requisition

A sample bar requisition, Form 10, is included in this section. The requisition form indicates sales value as well as the unit cost. The use of sales value is explained later. The form is otherwise self-explanatory.

## Inventory Form

Inventory-taking can be a problem often looked upon as a less-than-challenging task. However, accurate, timely inventories must be taken to achieve good control. Most problems develop from poorly organized storerooms, improper inventory techniques and poorly designed inventory forms.

Form 11 provides columns for three beverage locations per page. Proper use of the columns will greatly facilitate the inventory process. The usage is:

| | |
|---|---|
| Column 1 | Bottle Size |
| Column 2 | Description |
| Column 3 | Price at Cost |
| Columns 4, 5, 6 | Locations, i.e., Bar 1, Bar 2, Storeroom |
| Q = quantity; amount = (price x quantity) | |

The classification of the beverage inventory should be by standard groupings (i.e., scotch, bourbon, blends or gin). Each additional classification should be started on a new page, making it easier to total the inventory by classification. Furthermore, bottles should be listed alphabetically by brand and always kept in the same shelf or location.

The same inventory form is used in taking bar inventories. Arranging all bottles (on top of the bar, for example) by beverage classification and by alphabetical listing will greatly speed this process. Other techniques and pitfalls of inventory-taking should be studied in the various books on the subject.

# Bar Requisition

Day _____ Date _____ Bar Location _____

| List No. | Quantity | Size | Description | Unit Cost | Total Cost | Unit Sales Value | Total Sales Values |
|----------|----------|------|-------------|-----------|------------|------------------|--------------------|
|          |          |      |             |           |            |                  |                    |
|          |          |      |             |           |            |                  |                    |
|          |          |      |             |           |            |                  |                    |
|          |          |      |             |           |            |                  |                    |
|          |          |      |             |           |            |                  |                    |
|          |          |      |             |           |            |                  |                    |
|          |          |      |             |           |            |                  |                    |
|          |          |      |             |           |            |                  |                    |
|          |          |      |             |           |            |                  |                    |
|          |          |      |             |           |            |                  |                    |
|          |          |      |             |           |            |                  |                    |
|          |          |      |             |           |            |                  |                    |

Ordered by: _____ Issued by: _____ Received by: _____

# Beverage Inventory

DATE _____ PAGE _____

| 1<br><br>Size | 2<br><br>Item | 3<br><br>Price | 4<br>(Location) | | 5<br>(Location) | | 6<br>(Location) | |
|---|---|---|---|---|---|---|---|---|
| | | | Q | Amount | Q | Amount | Q | Amount |
| | | | | | | | | |
| | | | | | | | | |
| | | | | | | | | |
| | | | | | | | | |
| | | | | | | | | |
| | | | | | | | | |
| | | | | | | | | |
| | | | | | | | | |
| | | | | | | | | |
| | | | | | | | | |
| | | | | | | | | |
| | | | | | | | | |
| | | | | | | | | |
| | | | | | | | | |
| | | | | | | | | |
| | | | | | | | | |
| | | | | | | | | |
| | | | | | | | | |
| | | | | | | | | |
| TOTAL THIS PAGE | | | | | | | | |

# Perpetual Inventory

A perpetual-inventory record should be maintained on every item in the stockroom so that the physical counts at the end of each month can be compared with the balances shown on the respective account cards. Any differences should be immediately investigated. These perpetual-inventory records permit the spot-checking of the count of any item during the month, if desired.

There are numerous manual perpetual-inventory forms and systems available. The criteria for the system selected are: cards are designed to be used for six months to one year without rewriting, cards are easily accessible for posting, and all cards are well-bound and portable. For a small bar operation, a three-ring notebook with columnar paper will suffice. In larger restaurants, perpetual-inventory records are kept by computer. This process provides all the information quickly with a minimum of clerical effort.

## Summary of Beverage Cost and Sales, Par Stock

Form 12, the summary of beverage cost and sales, illustrates the daily and cumulative to-date cost and sales summary for the bar operation. In order for the daily cost to approximate the actual cost of merchandise consumed, it is advisable to establish a par stock for each item at the bar and to replace the empty bottles daily. In this manner, the daily issue to the bar will restore the stock to the par level and approximately represent the merchandise sold on the preceding day. A brief description of the purpose of each column follows.

## Column 1—Beverage Issues

Issues are the cost value of beverage requisitioned from the storeroom; the total will be from all the Form 10s used that day.

## Column 2—Food Transfers

This column represents the cost value of food used in mixed drinks. The cost includes fruit juices, lemons, oranges, pineapple, maraschino cherries, olives, cocktail onions and similar food issued from the kitchen or food storeroom on a food issue slip.

## Columns 3 and 4—Beverage Cost Today and To-Date

Beverage issues, plus food transfers, equal the cost for the day. This daily cost added to the to-date cost produces a new to-date cost.

## Columns 5 and 6—Beverage Sales Today and To-Date

Beverage sales are entered in Column 5 as taken from the restaurant daily report. The to-date sales are obtained by adding sales to prior sales.

## Columns 7 and 8—Cost Ratio to Sales Today and To-Date

The today ratio is calculated by dividing today's cost, column 3, by today's sales, column 5. The to-date ratio is obtained by dividing the to-date cost, column 4, by the to-date sales, column 6.

This form of cost and sales reporting is a minimum effort but may be sufficient for many bar operations, providing action is taken when the ratios differ from the standards.

Form 12

# Summary of Beverage Cost and Sales

For Month of _____, 19____

| Date | (1) Beverage Issues | (2) Food Transfers | (3) Beverage Cost Today | (4) Beverage Cost To-Date | (5) Beverage Sales Today | (6) Beverage Sales To-Date | (7) Cost Ratio to Sales Today | (8) Cost Ratio to Sales To-Date |
|---|---|---|---|---|---|---|---|---|
|  |  |  |  |  |  |  |  |  |
|  |  |  |  |  |  |  |  |  |
|  |  |  |  |  |  |  |  |  |
|  |  |  |  |  |  |  |  |  |
|  |  |  |  |  |  |  |  |  |
|  |  |  |  |  |  |  |  |  |
|  |  |  |  |  |  |  |  |  |
|  |  |  |  |  |  |  |  |  |
|  |  |  |  |  |  |  |  |  |
|  |  |  |  |  |  |  |  |  |
| TOTALS |  |  |  |  |  |  |  |  |

## Bar Cost and Storeroom Recapitulation

Many restaurants have more than one bar. In this situation operators usually prefer to maintain separate costs for each bar. A service bar may sell only bottled beverages, such as wine and champagne, while a public bar may serve mostly mixed drinks. The costs under these circumstances would be different in each bar. Since each bar should produce a cost based on a predetermined standard, each should be measured separately.

Form 13 is a bar cost and storeroom recapitulation report which was designed for a two-bar operation. Requisitions are used to accumulate the cost of the issues to each bar. Direct purchases represent merchandise which is not requisitioned, such as pressurized soft-drink containers and contents, keg beer and possibly some wines (where refrigerated storerooms are not available).

The total of the issues (requisitions) is adjusted by the opening and closing inventories. The total cost for the period is divided by the sales for the same period to obtain the cost ratio. The cost of the two bars, plus any storeroom difference, will reflect the total bar cost.

Food is requisitioned from the kitchen or food storeroom for use in mixed drinks. The report can be made weekly, bimonthly or monthly and can be based solely on issues as adjusted by the inventories whenever taken.

On Form 13, there is also a place for the reconciliation of the storeroom inventory. This is done by adding purchases to the opening inventory, then subtracting the storeroom issues. The result of this exercise is the estimated value of the remaining storeroom stock. The estimated inventory when compared with the actual storeroom inventory will usually reveal differences. These differences should be investigated if they are significant in the opinion of the management. The perpetual inventory will reveal where any differences occurred.

A place is also provided on Form 13 for calculating the adjusted cost, which would include any storeroom differences which may have occurred.

# Bar Cost and Storeroom Recapitulation

PERIOD

| BARS | Cost of Beverage | Actual Beverage Sales | COST PER DOLLAR SALES | |
|---|---|---|---|---|
| | | | This Period | Last Period |
| FRONT BAR | | | | |
| Opening Inventory | $_____ | | | |
| Add Issues- Issues/Direct/Food | _____ | | | |
| Subtotal | _____ | | | |
| Less Closing Inventory | | | | |
| Total Cost for Period | $ | $ | % | % |
| SERVICE BAR | | | | |
| Opening Inventory | $_____ | | | |
| Add Issues- Issues/Direct/Food | _____ | | | |
| Subtotal | _____ | | | |
| Less Closing Inventory | | | | |
| Total Cost for Period | $ | $ | % | % |
| Total Combined Bars | $ | $ | % | % |

## STOREROOM RECAPITULATION

| STOREROOM | Amount |
|---|---|
| Opening Inventory | $ |
| Add Purchases (Storeroom only) | |
| Subtotal | |
| Less Issues:  Front | |
| Service | |
| Kitchen | |
| Total | |
| Estimated Closing Inventory | |
| Actual Closing Inventory | |
| Difference | $ |

## ADJUSTED COSTS

| | Amount |
|---|---|
| Opening Inventory | $ |
| Add: Purchases-Store Purchases-Direct | |
| Total | |
| Deduct: Closing Inventory | |
| Cost of Sales | $ |
| RATIOS | |
| Actual | % |
| Estimated | % |
| | |
| Difference | % |

### Sales Value as a Cost Control

Some bars are controlled by calculating the sales value of the daily issues to the bar and thus arriving at a daily and monthly overage and shortage as compared with the actual bar sales. This is done by calculating the number of drinks per bottle issued, based on the standard sizes of drinks sold, multiplied by the beverage list prices. The sample bar requisition, Form 10, has columns for the unit selling value and total sales value. If this type of control is designed, Form 10 can be used for the dual purpose of estimating sales value and beverage cost.

The actual sales by classification of beverages may be taken from cash register data where the register is appropriately programmed, as most are. Some operators classify champagne, wines, whiskeys, gin, vodka, rum, brandy and more.

Many operators prefer to classify beverage sales into only the following: liquor, wine, beer and soft drinks. Some operators are content to make a simple division of sales and costs into a few major categories: mixed drinks and cocktails, beer and ale, wines, soft drinks and bottle sales.

The profit potential on each of these divisions of beverage sales is different and depends on the size of the drink and the prices charged. Thus, the total costs may be affected by the fluctuation in the proportion of sales in each group.

Sales value is a control that needs the advice and assistance of someone familiar with beverage cost-control procedures if it is to be effective. It is advisable to have professional advice in setting up and using this type of control.

Regardless of the method used, it is important that some form of control be established over even the smallest operation. The important point is that cost ratios obtained by the use of the illustrated reports or any other cost report are based on issues and are not adjusted by actual inventories until taken. When the exact cost is known, it must be compared with standards previously determined by the restaurant operator, with competitors' costs, if known, with previous periods, or industry standards. Timely and appropriate action by management to investigate unusual results is always required.

# Salaries and Wages Cost Control

Cost of salaries and wages is the second of the two major cost elements in restaurants. Control of this expense is the function of management, based on accurate reporting of hours worked and pay earned. Measurement of the expense is done by comparison with predetermined standards, forecasts, prior periods, industry studies or a combination of these bases.

Effective control depends upon good personnel management. To measure performance against standards, a restaurant operator must have established objectives and goals for the business and must carefully follow through with the following:

A. Job descriptions —Written objectives, goals and a full description of what is expected from the position are essential.

B. Hiring practices —Interviewing and screening candidates and then clearly defining the job, pay, vacation, meals and other benefits are good hiring practices.

C. Training and —Since most training is on-the-job, written instructions supervision and supervision for each task are necessary.

D. Scheduling —Schedules must be carefully charted and posted for employees to see. The system should be flexible enough so that the number of hours can be reduced when necessary.

E. Time recording —A time clock and time cards are the most common means of recording hours worked.

Determining the restaurant concept, goals and objectives, and the other functions listed on the previous page are not subjects of this text; however, effective control is difficult to administer without establishing the basic procedures. Information on these functions is available in books and pamphlets published by the National Restaurant Association and others. Salary and wage control begins with the time-recording function.

## Time Recording

Time card systems require the use of a time clock, a time card for each employee and a time card storage rack. Employees check in and out by stamping their cards when they begin and end their shifts. The employee's name and job position are written at the top of the time card.

Time cards are collected by a bookkeeper, payroll clerk or manager at the end of the payroll period. The hourly rate is added, and the time is approved by a person in authority. Many restaurant operators require supervisors to approve each card as employees check out.

## Salaries and Wage Worksheet and Check Register (Form 4)

Form 4 was described in a previous section of this text under "Simplified Record Keeping." The hours worked and the pay rate are recorded on this form by a bookkeeper or management person from information contained on the time cards.

The employees should be listed according to the selected departments and by their positions within their departments. The hours and salary expense are totaled by departments. Typical departmental breakdowns are preparation, sanitation, bar, service, and administration/management. The most appropriate employee categories are those that group similar functions in accordance with a uniform format.

## Control Reports (Form 14)

Employee data by category are summarized on the Form 4 worksheet by taking subtotals of the departments and groups within departments. The summarized data are then transferred to a usable report form which has parallel columns for insertion of comparative data. Form 14 has three columns: one for the current period, a second for the last period and a third for a measurement standard. Any comparative data may be used. One column could be used to accumulate to-date figures. This form illustrates only one of many comparative formats.

The three columns on Form 14 are used to report the hours worked and the corresponding expense for each group of employees and for each department.

The manager or supervisor compares the hours worked by position and by department with the prior period and with the predetermined standard. Differences should be reconciled and action taken, as required.

In addition to line-by-line comparisons, the statistics at the bottom of the form include the ratio to sales, productivity ratio and average sales per employee. These are the common measurements of payroll expense, and they provide an overview of the total operation.

# Salaries and Wages Control Report

Period Ending _____

| Sales this Period | This Period | | Last Period | | Standard | |
|---|---|---|---|---|---|---|
| $ | Hrs | Amount | Hrs | Amount | Hrs | Amount |
| Service: | | $ | | $ | | $ |
|   Servers | | | | | | |
|   Bus persons | | | | | | |
|   Oyster bar | | | | | | |
|    Total Service | | | | | | |
| Bartenders | | | | | | |
| Preparation: | | | | | | |
|   Manager | | | | | | |
|   Cook | | | | | | |
|   Preparation | | | | | | |
|    Total Preparation | | | | | | |
| Sanitation: | | | | | | |
|   Warewashers | | | | | | |
|   Cleaners | | | | | | |
|    Total Sanitation | | | | | | |
| Administration: | | | | | | |
|   Manager | | | | | | |
|   Cashiers | | | | | | |
|   Payroll Clerk | | | | | | |
|   Other | | | | | | |
|    Total Administration | | | | | | |
| Total Salaries and Wages | | | | | | |

| | | |
|---|---|---|
| Ratio to Sales | % | % | % |
| Productivity Ratio | % | % | % |
| Sales Per Employee | $ | $ | $ |

# APPENDIX A

## Sample Chart of Accounts Based on Uniform System of Accounts for Restaurants

The chart of accounts is a numbering system for the income and expense classifications conforming to the *Uniform System of Accounts for Restaurants*. The codes used here are not the only method for classifying the accounts; however, this is an acceptable standard grouping used by many restaurants.  The illustrated code-numbering system is designed to be flexible and to be added to or reduced to fit the requirements of the individual restaurant owner.  Some type of account code-numbering system must be used.

The listing that follows is intended to be quite comprehensive. Most restaurants will not require all of the account categories listed. If an account is used very rarely (or never), it should not be included in the chart of accounts. Use of fewer accounts definitely results in less complication.

# CHART OF ACCOUNTS

## ASSETS (1000)

| Account Number | Account Name |
| --- | --- |
| 1100 | Cash |
| 1110 | Change funds |
| 1120 | Cash on deposit |
| | |
| 1200 | Accounts receivable |
| 1210 | Customers |
| 1220 | Allowances and complimentaries |
| 1230 | Other |
| 1240 | Employees' loans and advances |
| 1250 | Provision for doubtful accounts |
| | |
| 1300 | Inventories |
| 1310 | Food |
| 1320 | Beverages |
| 1330 | Supplies |
| 1340 | Other |
| | |
| 1400 | Prepaid expenses |
| 1410 | Insurance |
| 1420 | Deposits |
| 1430 | Taxes |
| 1440 | Licenses |
| | |
| 1500 | Fixed assets |
| 1510 | Land |
| 1520 | Building |
| 1530 | Accumulated depreciation–building |
| 1540 | Leasehold improvements |
| 1550 | Accumulated amortization of improvements |
| 1560 | Furniture, fixtures and equipment (including POS equipment) |
| 1570 | Accumulated depreciation–furniture and equipment |
| 1580 | Automobiles/trucks |
| 1590 | Accumulated depreciation–automobiles/trucks |
| | |
| 1600 | Deferred charges |
| 1610 | Marketing program prepaid |
| 1620 | Pre-opening expenses |

## LIABILITIES (2000)

| | |
| --- | --- |
| 2100 | Payables |
| 2110 | Notes payable |
| 2120 | Accounts payable |
| 2200 | Taxes withheld and accrued |
| 2210 | Income Tax |
| 2220 | FICA |

| 2230 | Federal unemployment tax |
| 2240 | State unemployment tax |
| 2250 | Sales tax |
| 2260 | Employer's share of payroll taxes |
| 2270 | City taxes |
| 2300 | Accrued expenses |
| 2310 | Rent |
| 2320 | Payroll |
| 2330 | Interest |
| 2340 | Water |
| 2350 | Gas |
| 2360 | Electricity |
| 2370 | Personal property taxes |
| 2380 | Vacation |
| 2390 | Other |
| 2400 | Long-term debt |
| 2410 | Mortgage debt |
| 2420 | Capital leases |
| 2430 | Other debt |

## SHAREHOLDERS' EQUITY (3000)

| 3100 | Common stock |
| 3200 | Capital in excess of par |
| 3300 | Retained earnings |

## SALES (4000)

| 4100 | Food |
| 4200 | Beverages |

## COST OF SALES (5000)
## (Detailed sub-accounts, if desired, will vary by type of restaurant)

| 5100 | Cost of sales–food |
| 5200 | Cost of sales–beverages |

## OTHER INCOME (6000)

| 6100 | Cover charges and minimums |
| 6200 | Commissions |
| 6210 | Gift shop operation–net |
| 6220 | Telephone commissions |
| 6230 | Concessions |
| 6240 | Vending machine/game revenue |
| 6300 | Salvage and waste sales |
| 6400 | Cash discounts |
| 6500 | Meeting/banquet room rental |
| 6900 | Miscellaneous |

## OPERATING EXPENSES (7000)

| | |
|---|---|
| 7100 | Salaries and wages |
| 7105 | Service |
| 7110 | Preparation |
| 7115 | Sanitation |
| 7120 | Beverages |
| 7125 | Administrative |
| 7130 | Purchasing and storing |
| 7135 | Other |
| 7200 | Employee benefits |
| 7205 | FICA |
| 7210 | Federal unemployment tax |
| 7215 | State unemployment tax |
| 7220 | Workmen's compensation |
| 7225 | Group insurance |
| 7230 | State health insurance tax |
| 7235 | Welfare plan payments |
| 7240 | Pension plan payments |
| 7245 | Accident and health insurance premiums |
| 7250 | Hospitalization, Blue Cross, Blue Shield |
| 7255 | Employee meals |
| 7260 | Employee instruction and education expenses |
| 7265 | Employee Christmas and other parties |
| 7270 | Employee sports activities |
| 7275 | Medical expenses |
| 7280 | Credit union |
| 7285 | Awards and prizes |
| 7290 | Transportation and housing |
| 7300 | Occupancy costs |
| 7305 | Rent—minimum or fixed |
| 7310 | Percentage rent |
| 7315 | Ground rental |
| 7320 | Equipment rental |
| 7325 | Real estate taxes |
| 7330 | Personal property taxes |
| 7335 | Other municipal taxes |
| 7340 | Franchise tax |
| 7345 | Capital stock tax |
| 7350 | Partnership or corporation license fees |
| 7360 | Insurance on building and contents |
| 7370 | Depreciation |
| 7371 | Buildings |
| 7372 | Amortization of leasehold |
| 7373 | Amortization of leasehold improvements |
| 7374 | Furniture, fixtures and equipment |
| 7400 | Direct operating expenses |
| 7402 | Uniforms |
| 7404 | Laundry and dry cleaning |
| 7406 | Linen rental |
| 7408 | Linen |
| 7410 | China and glassware |

| | |
|---|---|
| 7412 | Silverware |
| 7414 | Kitchen utensils |
| 7416 | Auto and truck expense |
| 7418 | Cleaning supplies |
| 7420 | Paper supplies |
| 7422 | Guest supplies |
| 7424 | Bar supplies |
| 7426 | Menus and wine lists |
| 7428 | Contract cleaning |
| 7430 | Exterminating |
| 7432 | Flowers and decorations |
| 7436 | Parking lot expenses |
| 7438 | Licenses and permits |
| 7440 | Banquet expenses |
| 7498 | Other operating expenses |
| 7500 | Music and entertainment |
| 7505 | Musicians |
| 7510 | Professional entertainers |
| 7520 | Mechanical music |
| 7525 | Contracted wire services |
| 7530 | Piano rental and tuning |
| 7535 | Films, records, tapes and sheet music |
| 7540 | Programs |
| 7550 | Royalties to ASCAP, BMI |
| 7555 | Booking agents fees |
| 7560 | Meals served to musicians |
| 7600 | Marketing |
| 7601 | Selling and promotion |
| 7602 | Sales representative service |
| 7603 | Travel expense on solicitation |
| 7604 | Direct mail |
| 7605 | Telephone used for advertising and promotion |
| 7606 | Complimentary food and beverage (including gratis meals to customers) |
| 7607 | Postage |
| 7610 | Advertising |
| 7611 | Newspaper |
| 7612 | Magazines and trade journals |
| 7613 | Circulars, brochures, postal cards and other mailing pieces |
| 7614 | Outdoor signs |
| 7615 | Radio and television |
| 7616 | Programs, directories and guides |
| 7617 | Preparation of copy, photographs, etc. |
| 7620 | Public relations and publicity |
| 7621 | Civic and community projects |
| 7622 | Donations |
| 7623 | Souvenirs, favors, treasure chest items |
| 7630 | Fees and commissions |
| 7631 | Advertising or promotional agency fees |
| 7640 | Research |
| 7641 | Travel in connection with research |
| 7642 | Outside research agency |

| | |
|---|---|
| 7643 | Product testing |
| 7700 | Utilities |
| 7705 | Electric current |
| 7710 | Electric bulbs |
| 7715 | Water |
| 7720 | Removal of waste |
| 7725 | Other fuel |
| 7800 | Administrative and general expenses |
| 7805 | Office stationery, printing and supplies |
| 7810 | Data processing costs |
| 7815 | Postage |
| 7820 | Telegrams and telephone |
| 7825 | Dues and subscriptions |
| 7830 | Traveling expenses |
| 7835 | Insurance—general |
| 7840 | Commissions on credit card charges |
| 7845 | Provision for doubtful accounts |
| 7850 | Cash over or (short) |
| 7855 | Professional fees |
| 7860 | Protective and bank pick-up services |
| 7865 | Bank charges |
| 7870 | Miscellaneous |
| 7900 | Repairs and maintenance |
| 7902 | Furniture and fixtures |
| 7904 | Kitchen equipment |
| 7906 | Office equipment |
| 7908 | Refrigeration |
| 7910 | Air conditioning |
| 7912 | Plumbing and heating |
| 7914 | Electrical and mechanical |
| 7916 | Floors and carpets |
| 7918 | Buildings |
| 7920 | Parking lot |
| 7922 | Gardening and grounds maintenance |
| 7924 | Building alterations |
| 7928 | Painting, plastering and decorating |
| 7990 | Maintenance contracts |
| 7996 | Autos and trucks |
| 7998 | Other equipment and supplies |

## INTEREST AND CORPORATE OVERHEAD (8000)

| | |
|---|---|
| 8100 | Interest |
| 8105 | Notes payable |
| 8110 | Long-term debt |
| 8115 | Other |
| 8200 | Corporate or Executive Office overhead |
| 8205 | Officers' salaries |
| 8210 | Directors' salaries |
| 8215 | Corporate office payroll |
| 8220 | Corporate office employee benefits |
| 8225 | Corporate office rent |

| 8230 | Corporate travel and entertainment |
|------|-----------------------------------|
| 8235 | Corporate office automobile expense |
| 8240 | Corporate office insurance |
| 8245 | Corporate office utilities |
| 8250 | Corporate office data processing |
| 8255 | Legal and accounting expense |
| 8260 | Corporate miscellaneous expense |

## INCOME TAX (9000)

| 9000 | Income Taxes |
|------|--------------|
| 9010 | Federal |
| 9020 | State |

# APPENDIX B

## Expense Dictionary

This dictionary is designed to help the restaurant operation classify expenses in accordance with the *Uniform System of Accounts for Restaurants*. There are certain expenditures that should not be recorded as expenses but should be capitalized on the balance sheet. Capitalized items are included on the balance sheet as assets and are depreciated or amortized over time. Examples of these expenditures which should be capitalized include those for property and equipment, those for repairs that extend the life of an asset, and certain interest costs incurred during the construction of assets. Operators should refer to the applicable accounting principles for these areas for guidance or contact their accountants.

The following abbreviations are used in this dictionary:

G&A—General and Administrative expense
R&M—Repairs and Maintenance expense

### A

| | |
|---|---|
| Accountants' Fees | G&A—Professional Fees |
| Adding Machine—Service | G&A—Office Stationery, Printing & Supplies |
| Adding Machine—Tapes | G&A—Office Stationery, Printing & Supplies |
| Advertising Agency Fees | Marketing—Fees & Commissions |
| Advertising—Direct Mail | Marketing—Selling & Promotion |
| Advertising—Novelties | Marketing—Public Relations & Publicity |
| Advertising—Outdoor | Marketing—Advertising |
| Advertising—Publications | Marketing—Advertising |
| Advertising—Radio & TV | Marketing—Advertising |
| Air Conditioning Systems Repairs | R&M—Repairs to Air Conditioning |
| Air Express Charges. | G&A—Miscellaneous |
| Alarm Service—Fire or Burglar | G&A—Protective Service |
| Aluminum Trays | Direct Operating Expenses—Tableware, Linen |
| Amortization—Bond Discount | Interest Expense |
| Amortization—Bond Expense | Interest Expense |
| Amortization—Financing Costs | Interest Expense |
| Amortization—Leasehold | Depreciation/Amortization of Leasehold |
| Amortization—Leasehold Improvements | Depreciation/Amortization of Leasehold Improvements |
| Appetizers—Bar | Direct Operating Expenses—Bar |
| Aprons | Direct Operating Expenses—Uniforms |
| Ash Trays—China & Glass | Direct Operating Expenses—Tableware, Linen |
| Association Dues | G&A—Dues & Subscriptions |
| Athletic Equipment for Employees | Employee Benefits—Other Expenses |
| Attorney's Fees | G&A—Professional Fees |
| Awards—Employees | Employee Benefits—Other Expenses |

## B

| | |
|---|---|
| Bad Debts .......................................... | G&A—Provision for Doubtful Accounts |
| Badges .............................................. | Direct Operating Expenses—Uniforms |
| Bar Utensils ....................................... | Direct Operating Expenses—Supplies, Bar |
| Batter Bowls....................................... | Direct Operating Expenses—Kitchen Utensils |
| Beaters.............................................. | Direct Operating Expenses—Kitchen Utensils |
| Beeper Rental ..................................... | G&A—Telephone |
| Beepers—Patron.................................. | Direct Operating Expenses—Supplies, Guest |
| Beverage Licenses ............................... | Direct Operating Expenses—Licenses, Permits |
| Beverage Lists ..................................... | Direct Operating Expenses—Menus, Drink Lists |
| Beverage Mixers .................................. | Direct Operating Expenses—Supplies, Bar |
| Beverage Signs .................................... | Direct Operating Expenses—Menus, Drink Lists |
| Beverage Spoons ................................. | Direct Operating Expenses—Supplies |
| Beverage Stirrers—Glass....................... | Direct Operating Expenses—Supplies |
| Beverage Taxes.................................... | G&A—Sales Tax |
| Billboards........................................... | Marketing—Advertising |
| Boiler Explosion Insurance..................... | G&A—Insurance (General) |
| Boiler Gauges...................................... | Utility Services—Engineer's Supplies |
| Boiler Inspection.................................. | R&M—Repairs to Plumbing & Heating/Electrical |
| Boiler Repairs ..................................... | R&M—Repairs to Plumbing & Heating |
| Bond Discount...................................... | Interest Expense |
| Bond Expense Amortization.................... | Interest Expense |
| Bond Interest....................................... | Interest Expense |
| Bonuses—Employees ............................ | Salaries & Wages |
| Book Matches (Guest) ........................... | Direct Operating Expenses—Supplies, Guest Supplies |
| Books—Account ................................... | G&A—Office Stationery, Printing & Supplies |
| Books—Records ................................... | G&A—Office Stationery, Printing & Supplies |
| Bowls—Batter, Mixing........................... | Direct Operating Expenses—Kitchen Utensils |
| Bowls—China, Glass, Salad................... | Direct Operating Expenses—Tableware, Linen |
| Boxes—Pastry ..................................... | Direct Operating Expenses—Supplies, Paper |
| Boxes—To Go ...................................... | Direct Operating Expenses—Supplies, Paper |
| Brooms .............................................. | Direct Operating Expenses—Supplies, Cleaning |
| Brushes—Cleaning ............................... | Direct Operating Expenses—Supplies, Cleaning |
| Building Depreciation ........................... | Depreciation |
| Building Insurance ............................... | Insurance on Buildings & Contents (Occupancy Costs) |
| Building Repairs................................... | R&M Buildings |
| Burglar Alarm Service........................... | G&A Protective Services |
| Burglary Insurance ............................... | G&A Insurance (General) |

## C

| | |
|---|---|
| Cable TV–Rental................................... | Occupancy Costs—Equipment Rental |
| Can Openers....................................... | Direct Operating Expenses—Kitchen Utensils |
| Candles .............................................. | Direct Operating Expenses—Tableware, Linen |
| Candlesticks—China............................. | Direct Operating Expenses—Tableware, Linen |
| Carafes.............................................. | Direct Operating Expenses—Tableware, Linen |
| Carpet Repairs.................................... | R&M—Floors & Floor Coverings |
| Carpet & Rugs—Cleaning ..................... | Direct Operating Expenses—Laundry, Dry Cleaning |

| | |
|---|---|
| Cash Overage & Shortage | G&A—Cash Shortages |
| Cash Register—Repairs | R&M—Office Equipment |
| Cash Register Supplies | G&A—Office Stationery, Printing & Supplies |
| Cashier Forms | G&A—Office Stationery, Printing & Supplies |
| Ceiling Repairs | R&M—Plastering or Building |
| Cellophane | Direct Operating Expenses—Supplies, Paper |
| Cellular Phone—Business Use | G&A—Telephone |
| Cellular Phone—Patron Use | Direct Operating Expenses—Supplies, Guest |
| Chair Rentals—Banquets | Direct Operating Expenses—Banquet Expense |
| Chair Rentals—Non-Banquets | Occupancy Costs, Equipment Rental |
| Checks—Bank | G&A—Office Stationery, Printing, Supplies |
| Checks—Restaurant | G&A—Office Stationery, Printing, Supplies |
| Checks—Waiter | G&A—Office Stationery, Printing, Supplies |
| China | Direct Operating Expense—Tableware, Linen |
| Christmas Gifts—Employees | Employee Benefits—Other Expenses, Christmas & Other Parties |
| Christmas Gifts—Other Than Employees | Marketing—Public Relations & Publicity |
| Christmas Trees & Decorations | Direct Operating Expenses—Flowers, Decorations |
| Civic & Community Project | Marketing—Public Relations & Publicity |
| Cleaning Fluids | Direct Operating Expenses—Supplies, Cleaning |
| Cleaning Rags | Direct Operating Expenses—Supplies, Cleaning |
| Cleaning Supplies | Direct Operating Expenses—Supplies, Cleaning |
| Clipboards | G&A—Office Stationery, Printing & Supplies |
| Cocktail Napkins—Paper | Direct Operating Expenses—Supplies, Paper |
| Cocktail Shakers | Direct Operating Expenses—Supplies, Bar |
| Coffee (Free) | Marketing—Selling & Promotion, Entertainment Costs |
| Coffee Pots | Direct Operating Expenses—Tableware, Linen |
| Coffee Urn Repairs | R&M—Kitchen Equipment |
| Coin Bags | G&A—Office Stationery, Printing & Supplies |
| Coin Wrappers | G&A—Office Stationery, Printing & Supplies |
| Collars | Direct Operating Expenses—Uniforms |
| Complimentary Beverage | Marketing—Selling & Promotion, Entertainment Costs |
| Complimentary Beverage—Musicians & Entertainers | Music—Entertainment & Meals |
| Complimentary Food | Marketing—Selling, Promotion & Entertainment Costs |
| Complimentary Food—Musicians & Entertainers | Music—Entertainment & Meals |
| Complimentary Parking | Marketing—Selling & Promotion, Entertainment Costs |
| Computer Network Subcription Fees | G&A—Data Processing |
| Computer/PC Software | Direct Operating Expenses—Computer Software |
| Computer/PC Service / Repairs | R&M—Computer |
| Computer Rentals | G&A—Data Processing Costs |
| Consultant Fees, Professional | G&A—Professional Fees |
| Containers—Liquid, Paper | Direct Operating Expenses—Supplies, Paper |
| Contract Cleaning | Direct Operating Expenses—Contract Cleaning |
| Contract Entertainment | Music & Entertainment—Professional Entertainers |
| Contract Exterminating | Direct Operating Expenses—Contract Cleaning |
| Contributions | Marketing—Public Relations & Publicity |

## H

## I

## K

| | |
|---|---|
| Knives—Silver ........................................ | Direct Operating Expenses—Tableware, Linen |

## L

| | |
|---|---|
| Ladles—Kitchen..................................... | Direct Operating Expenses—Tableware, Linen, Silverware |
| Landscaping .......................................... | R&M—Landscaping |
| Laundry.................................................. | Direct Operating Expenses—Laundry, Dry cleaning |
| Leasehold Amortization........................... | Depreciation—Amortization of Leasehold |
| Leasehold Improvements Amortization ..... | Depreciation—Amortization of Leasehold Improvements |
| Legal Expenses ..................................... | G&A—Professional Fees |
| Legal Fees ............................................ | G&A—Professional Fees |
| Licenses—Liquor, Federal ....................... | Direct Operating Expenses—Licenses, Permits |
| Licenses—Beverages, Municipal.............. | Direct Operating Expenses—Licenses, Permits |
| Licenses—Beverages, State..................... | Direct Operating Expenses—Licenses, Permits |
| Licenses—General.................................. | Direct Operating Expenses—Licenses, Permits |
| Licenses—Music .................................... | Direct Operating Expenses—Licenses, Permits |
| Light—Cost of ....................................... | Utility Services—Electric |
| Linen..................................................... | Direct Operating Expenses—Tableware, Linen |
| Linen Napkins........................................ | Direct Operating Expenses—Tableware, Linen |
| Linen Rental .......................................... | Direct Operating Expenses—Linen Rental |
| Linen Towels ......................................... | Direct Operating Expenses—Tableware, Linen |
| Liquid Containers, Paper ........................ | Direct Operating Expenses—Supplies, Paper |
| Lock Repairs ......................................... | R&M—Buildings |
| Loss on Sale of Property......................... | Gain or Loss on Sale of Property |
| Lost & Damaged Articles (Guest) ............ | G&A—Claims & Damages Paid |

## M

| | |
|---|---|
| Machinery Repairs ................................. | R&M |
| Magazine Advertising ............................ | Marketing—Advertising |
| Magazines—Trade.................................. | G&A—Dues & Subscriptions |
| Maintenance Contracts—Electric Signs .... | Repairs & Maintenance |
| Maintenance Contracts— Office Equipment ............................. | Repairs & Maintenance |
| Management Fees................................... | Corporate Overhead |
| Manuals—Service (Instructional Materials) ......................................... | G&A—Office Stationery, Printing & Supplies |
| Manuals—Training ................................. | G&A—Office Stationery, Printing & Supplies |
| Market Research. .................................. | Marketing—Research |
| Marquee Licenses.................................. | Direct Operating Expenses—Licenses, Permits |
| Marquee Repairs.................................... | R&M—Buildings |
| Matches (Guest) .................................... | Direct Operating Expenses—Supplies, Guest |
| Meals—Employees ................................. | Employee Benefits—Meals |
| Membership Dues—Associations............. | G&A—Dues & Subscriptions |
| Menus.................................................... | Direct Operating Expenses—Menus, Drink Lists |
| Mixer Repairs ....................................... | R&M—Kitchen Equipment |
| Mixing Bowls......................................... | Direct Operating Expenses—Kitchen Utensils |
| Mixing Spoons....................................... | Direct Operating Expenses—Kitchen Utensils |
| Mops..................................................... | Direct Operating Expenses—Supplies, Cleaning |
| Mortgage Interest.................................. | Interest |

| | |
|---|---|
| Mouse Traps | Direct Operating Expenses—Supplies, Cleaning |
| Musicians | Music & Entertainment |
| Muzak | Music & Entertainment |

## N

| | |
|---|---|
| Napkins—Linen | Direct Operating Expenses—Tableware, Linen |
| Napkins—Paper | Direct Operating Expenses—Supplies, Paper |
| Napkins—Paper (Cocktail) | Direct Operating Expenses—Supplies, Paper |
| Newspaper Advertising | Marketing—Advertising |
| Newspapers (for Resale) | Other Income |
| Notary Fees | G&A—Professional Fees |
| Novelties (Advertising) | Marketing—Public Relations & Publicity |
| Nutritional Consulting | G&A—Professional Fees |

## O

| | |
|---|---|
| Office Equipment Repairs | R&M—Office Equipment |
| Office Supplies | G&A—Office Stationery, Printing & Supplies |
| Oil—Fuel | Utility Services—Fuel |
| Openers—Bottle | Direct Operating Expenses—Kitchen Utensils |
| Openers—Can | Direct Operating Expenses—Kitchen Utensils |
| Organization Expenses | G&A—Miscellaneous |
| Outdoor Advertising | Marketing—Advertising |
| Overages & Shortages—Cash | G&A—Cash Shortages |

## P

| | |
|---|---|
| Pager Rental | G&A—Telephone |
| Pails | Direct Operating Expenses—Supplies, Cleaning |
| Paint | R&M—Painting & Decorating |
| Paint Cleaner | Direct Operating Expenses—Supplies, Cleaning |
| Painting & Decorating | R&M—Painting & Decorating |
| Pans | Direct Operating Expenses—Kitchen Utensils |
| Paper Bags | Direct Operating Expenses—Supplies, Paper |
| Paper Clips | G&A—Office Stationery, Printing & Supplies |
| Paper—Cooking | Direct Operating Expenses—Supplies, Paper |
| Paper Cups | Direct Operating Expenses—Supplies, Paper |
| Paper Napkins | Direct Operating Expenses—Supplies, Paper |
| Paper Napkins—Cocktail | Direct Operating Expenses—Supplies, Paper |
| Paper Plates | Direct Operating Expenses—Supplies, Paper |
| Paper—Shelf | Direct Operating Expenses—Supplies, Paper |
| Paper Supplies—Food | Direct Operating Expenses—Supplies, Paper |
| Paper Towels (Employee) | Direct Operating Expenses—Supplies, Paper |
| Pastry Boxes | Direct Operating Expenses—Supplies, Paper |
| Pastry Tubes | Direct Operating Expenses—Kitchen Utensils |
| Payroll Service | G&A—Data Processing Costs |
| Pencils | G&A—Office Stationery, Printing & Supplies |
| Pencil Sharpeners | G&A—Office Stationery, Printing & Supplies |
| Pens | G&A—Office Stationery, Printing & Supplies |
| Pensions (Nonunion) | Employee Benefits—Insurance |

| | |
|---|---|
| Pensions (Union) | Employee Benefits—Insurance |
| Permits | Direct Operating Expenses—Licenses, Permits |
| Personal Prop. Taxes | Occupancy Costs—Personal Property Taxes |
| Piano Rentals—Banquet | Music & Entertainment |
| Piano Rentals—Dining Rooms | Music & Entertainment |
| Piano Tuning—Dining Rooms | Music & Entertainment |
| Pitchers | Direct Operating Expenses—Tableware, Linen |
| Pizza Boxes | Direct Operating Expenses—Supplies, Paper |
| Placards | Marketing—Advertising |
| Place Cards | Direct Operating Expenses—Miscellaneous |
| Plants | Direct Operating Expenses—Flowers, Decorations |
| Plates | Direct Operating Expenses—Tableware, Linen |
| Plates—Paper | Direct Operating Expenses—Supplies, Paper |
| Platters | Direct Operating Expenses—Tableware, Linen |
| Polish—Brass | Direct Operating Expenses—Supplies, Cleaning |
| Polish—Floor | Direct Operating Expenses—Supplies, Cleaning |
| Polish—Furniture | Direct Operating Expenses—Supplies, Cleaning |
| Polish—Metal | Direct Operating Expenses—Supplies, Cleaning |
| Post Office Box Rental | Miscellaneous |
| Postage | G&A—Postage |
| Postage Meter Rentals | G&A—Postage |
| Postage—for Promotional Mailings | Marketing—Selling & Promotion |
| Postcards—for Resale | Other Income |
| Pots | Direct Operating Expenses—Kitchen Utensils |
| Preopening Expenses | G&A |
| Printed Forms | G&A—Office Stationery, Printing & Supplies |
| Printed Matter—Advertising | Marketing—Advertising |
| Printing & Stationery | G&A—Office Stationery, Printing & Supplies |
| Prizes—Employee | Employee Benefits—Other Expenses |
| Professional Entertainers | Music & Entertainment |
| Protective Services | G&A—Protective Service |
| Provision for Doubtful Accounts | G&A—Provision for Doubtful Accts. |
| Public Address System Repairs | R&M—Electrical Systems |
| Public Relations | Marketing—Public Relations & Publicity |
| Publications—Patron Newsletter | Marketing—Advertising |

## R

| | |
|---|---|
| Radio Advertising | Marketing—Advertising |
| Rags—Cleaning | Direct Operating Expenses—Supplies, Cleaning |
| Real Estate Taxes | Occupancy Costs—Real Estate Taxes |
| Record Books | G&A—Office Stationery, Printing & Supplies |
| Recycling—Bins | Direct Operating Expenses—Supplies |
| Recycling—Pickup Fees | Direct Operating Expenses—Miscellaneous |
| Recycling—Revenues | Other Income—Salvage and Waste Sales |
| Refrigeration Repairs | R&M—Refrigeration |
| Refuse Removal | Utility Services—Removal of Waste |
| Rentals—Chairs | Occupancy |
| Rentals—Tables | Occupancy |
| Rentals—Piano | Occupancy |
| Rent—Building & Land | Occupancy Costs—Ground |
| Rent—Computer Equipment | G&A—Data Processing Costs |

| | |
|---|---|
| Replacement of Window Glass .............. | R&M—Building |
| Replating Silver .................................... | Direct Operating Expenses—Replacement of Silver |
| Reservation Forms ............................... | G&A—Office Stationery, Printing & Supplies |
| Restaurant Checks ............................... | G&A—Office Stationery, Printing & Supplies |
| Restaurant Signs .................................. | Marketing—Advertising |
| Rock Salt ............................................. | Repairs—Gardening and Ground Maintenance |
| Roof Repairs ....................................... | R&M—Roof |
| Rubber Bands ...................................... | G&A—Office Stationery, Printing & Supplies |
| Rubber Mats ........................................ | Direct Operating Expenses—Kitchen Utensils |
| Rubbish Removal .................................. | Utility Services—Removal of Waste |
| Rug Repairs ........................................ | R&M—Floors & Floor Coverings |

### S

| | |
|---|---|
| Safety Envelopes ................................. | G&A—Office Stationery, Printing, & Supplies |
| Salad Bowls ........................................ | Direct Operating Expenses—Tableware & Linen |
| Sales Tax ............................................. | G&A—Sales Taxes |
| Sani-Racks—Repairs ........................... | R&M |
| Saucers ............................................... | Direct Operating Expenses—Tableware, Linen |
| Scissors ............................................... | G&A—Office Stationery, Printing & Supplies |
| Scotch Tape ........................................ | G&A—Office Stationery, Printing & Supplies |
| Seating Lists ....................................... | G&A—Office Stationery, Printing & Supplies |
| Security—Contracted ........................... | G&A—Protective Services |
| Servers' Checks .................................. | G&A—Office Stationery, Printing & Supplies |
| Servers' Commissions ......................... | Salaries—Wages & Service |
| Service Manuals (Employee) ................. | G&A—Office Stationery, Printing & Supplies |
| Sewer System Repairs .......................... | R&M—Plumbing & Heating |
| Shakers—Beverage ............................. | Direct Operating Expenses—Supplies, Bar |
| Sharpeners—Pencil .............................. | G&A—Office Stationery, Printing & Supplies |
| Sharpening Knives .............................. | Direct Operating Expenses—Kitchen Utensils |
| Shelf Paper ......................................... | Direct Operating Expenses—Paper |
| Shortages & Overages—Cash ............... | G&A—Cash Shortages |
| Shrubbery ........................................... | R&M—Gardening & Grounds Maintenance |
| Sidewalk Repairs ................................ | R&M—Parking Lot Repairs |
| Sign Repairs ....................................... | R&M—Building |
| Signs—Beverages ............................... | Marketing—Advertising |
| Small Tools ......................................... | Utility Services—Engineers' Supplies |
| Snow Removal ..................................... | R&M—Gardening and Ground Maintenance |
| Soap for Cleaning ............................... | Direct Operating Expenses—Supplies, Cleaning |
| Soap (Guest) ....................................... | Direct Operating Expenses—Supplies, Guest |
| Soft Drinks—Food ............................... | Cost of Food |
| Sponges—Cleaning .............................. | Direct Operating Expenses—Supplies, Cleaning |
| Spoons—Beverage, Kitchen, Mixing ........ | Direct Operating Expenses—Kitchen Utensils |
| Spoons—Silver .................................... | Direct Operating Expenses—Tableware, Linen |
| Spotlight Rentals—Banquet .................... | Direct Operating Expenses—Banquet Expenses |
| Stairway Repairs ................................. | R&M—Building |
| Stamps—Advertising ............................. | Marketing—Advertising |
| Stamps—General ................................. | G&A—Postage |
| Staplers ............................................... | G&A—Office Stationery, Printing & Supplies |
| Staples ................................................ | G&A—Office Stationery, Printing & Supplies |
| State Income Taxes .............................. | Income Taxes |

State Unemployment Taxes ..................... Employee Benefits—Payroll Taxes
Stationery.............................................. G&A—Office Stationery, Printing & Supplies
Steel Wool ........................................... Direct Operating Expenses—Supplies, Cleaning
Sticks—Swizzle..................................... Direct Operating Expenses—Supplies, Bar
Stirrers, for Glasses ............................. Direct Operating Expenses—Supplies, Paper
Stock Transfer Agents Fees .................... G&A—Professional Fees
Storeroom Issue Reports ........................ G&A—Office Stationery, Printing & Supplies
Strainers—Bars .................................... Direct Operating Expenses—Supplies, Bar
Strainers—Beverages ............................ Direct Operating Expenses—Bar
Strainers—Kitchen ................................ Direct Operating Expenses—Kitchen Utensils
Straws.................................................. Direct Operating Expenses—Supplies, Paper
Straws—Bar ......................................... Direct Operating Expenses—Supplies, Bar
Subscriptions—Trade Publications ........... G&A—Dues & Subscriptions
Suggestion Awards—Employees ............. Employee Benefits—Other Expenses

## T

Table Clothes ....................................... Direct Operating Expenses—Tableware & Linen
Table Covers......................................... Direct Operating Expenses—Tableware & Linen
Table Tent Cards .................................. Direct Operating Expenses—Menus, Drink Lists
Taxes—Franchise................................... Income Taxes—Franchise Taxes
Taxes—Income ..................................... Income Taxes
Telephone Directory Advertising.............. Marketing—Advertising
Telephone Equipment Charges ............... G&A—Telephone
Telephone Rentals................................. G&A—Telephone
Television Repairs ................................. R&M—Electrical
Theater Program Advertising.................. Marketing—Advertising
Time Clock Repairs............................... R&M—Office Equipment
Toothpicks ........................................... Direct Operating Expenses—Supplies
Towels—Linen ...................................... Direct Operating Expenses—Tableware, Linen
Towels—Paper ...................................... Direct Operating Expenses—Supplies, Paper
Toys...................................................... Marketing—Selling & Promotion
Training Seminars.................................. G&A—Training Costs
Trays—Aluminum .................................. Direct Operating Expenses—Tableware, Linen
Trays—China, Glass or Silver ................. Direct Operating Expenses—Tableware, Linen
Tubes—Pastry ....................................... Direct Operating Expenses—Kitchen Utensils
Tumblers............................................... Direct Operating Expenses—Tableware, Linen
Typewriter Repairs................................. R&M—Office Equipment

## U

Uncollectible Accounts ........................... G&A—Provision for Doubtful Accounts
Uniforms .............................................. Direct Operating Expenses—Uniforms
Uniforms Cleaning................................. Direct Operating Expenses—Laundry, Dry Cleaning
Uniforms Laundering............................. Direct Operating Expenses—Laundry, Dry Cleaning
Uniforms Rental.................................... Direct Operating Expenses—Laundry, Dry Cleaning
Uniforms Repair ................................... Direct Operating Expenses—Laundry, Dry Cleaning
Utensils—Bar ....................................... Direct Operating Expenses—Supplies, Bar
Utensils—Kitchen.................................. Direct Operating Expenses—Kitchen Utensils

## V

## W